Football Weekends at Notre Dame

Football Weekends at
NOTRE

Written by
Bill Schmitt

Photography by
Lou Sabo

DAME

Snapshots and Traditions

University of Notre Dame Press

Notre Dame, Indiana

Copyright © 2008 by University of Notre Dame
Notre Dame, Indiana 46556
www.undpress.nd.edu
All Rights Reserved

Manufactured in the United States of America

Designed by Wendy McMillen;
set in 10.3/13.8 ITC Giovanni; printed on 60# Anthem White
Matte paper by Sheridan Books, Inc.

We gratefully acknowledge permission to use an image
from the motion picture *Rudy.* © 1993 TriStar Pictures, Inc.
All Rights Reserved. Courtesy of TriStar Pictures.

Library of Congress Cataloging-in-Publication Data
Schmitt, Bill.
Football weekends at Notre Dame : snapshots and
traditions / written by Bill Schmitt ; photography by
Lou Sabo.
    p. cm.
ISBN-13: 978-0-268-04129-8 (pbk. : alk. paper)
ISBN-10: 0-268-04129-6 (pbk. : alk. paper)
1. Notre Dame Fighting Irish (Football team)
2. University of Notre Dame—Football—History. I. Title.
GV958.N6S24   2008
796.332'630977289—dc22
                            2008006400

∞ *The paper in this book meets the guidelines for permanence
and durability of the Committee on Production Guidelines for
Book Longevity of the Council on Library Resources.*

CONTENTS

PREFACE

A Whole That's Bigger than Four Quarters

Every fall, hundreds of thousands of Notre Dame football fans observe their version of a "liturgical calendar" of feast days—a series of weekends for gathering in and around South Bend, Indiana, to enjoy a kind of communion. They have seen with their own eyes, perhaps as Notre Dame students, or as members of the Notre Dame family, or as its neighbors or its friends, that there are some things you don't have to be cynical about. There are some things you don't have to trivialize, or compartmentalize, or back away from as the other guy's definition of reality.

You can take Notre Dame football seriously because its context rings true. It dons an armor of glory, but it does not put on airs. It simultaneously affirms the personal narratives of individuals and groups. It's connected to good people, good purposes, good memories, and good times, along with imperfections, disappointments, painful sacrifices, and ongoing struggles. It's something big in which we can proudly and humbly share.

The story of Notre Dame football is a parable about relationships. The experience of gameday on the Notre Dame campus is a participation in a central truth recognized through both faith and reason: Everything is connected to everything else. Interactions abound between the wide variety of communities that congregate around the main event of the weekend. Immersed in crosscurrents of loyalty, people and groups find themselves linked to others involved with gameday in myriad ways:

- Students, whether or not they have any involvement on the field, join together to celebrate their own talents, their own sense of possibilities, and their own place in a world of traditions and communities (chapter 1).
- Catholics and believers of all faiths abandon any shyness about religion and joyfully integrate its symbols and practices into their day, allowing recreation to take on its meaning as re-creation (chapter 2).
- Alumni draw strength from nostalgia and enduring loyalties and can pass their love on to their families and friends—and total strangers (chapter 3).
- Visitors from around the country and around the world can receive a hospitality that does not force them into their usual roles as mere consumers, or spectators (chapter 4).
- Neighbors in the civic structure of local towns and cities like South Bend can feel pride about their backgrounds and can see economic and emotional benefits that boost their sense of rootedness and generosity (chapter 6).
- Athletes and their coaches and all those involved in the world of sport are reminded of the best fruits that physical competition can produce—life lessons about fairness, solidarity, sacrifice, tenacity, well-roundedness, a

striving for excellence, a capacity for heroism (chapter 7).

- People of all kinds find roles to play—and find them so rewarding that these roles become more inclusive and more other-centered, making their stories important only insofar as they signify the gifts one has for others (chapter 8).

These seven points constitute a touchstone (or touchdown!) of inclusiveness that the chapters of this book will convey. We will explore the traditions that have been allowed to flourish— and which continue to emerge—when people are encouraged to relate the present to the past, simple actions to deeper aspirations, serious principles to a sense of humor and sheer fun. We will explore the dynamic whereby communities of shared interest strengthen themselves by co-operating respectfully and creatively with other communities, in marked contrast to the modern cultural trend toward separatism and self-absorption.

We will implicitly explore the notion that all of this weekend brouhaha is one of Notre Dame's powerful ways to engage the culture, to inspire more excellent possibilities, to be salt for the earth (Matthew 5:13) that preserves good things and adds some spice. Engagement with culture was the unlikely story of Notre Dame's football team nearly a century ago, when it helped to give self-esteem to underdog immigrants, many of them Irish. Its message is still about how great an individual can be—and how great we can be together, given the right mix of pride and humility, triumph and sacrifice, personal dignity and communal sensibility.

This book's exploration of the traditions surrounding Notre Dame football, while grounded in the preceding reflection about the deeper meanings of gameday weekends and drawn from a combination of official university statements and individuals' unofficial recollections and reflections, will dwell mostly on the serious *fun* embodied by the people, places, and activities you will see here. Share in that fun. Be surprised by the joy. If Notre Dame football deals in incarnations of enlightenment and revelations of relationship, then we can honor it by huddling around its pictures and smiling at its stories.

We end this preface with a few words about what the book is *not*. It is not a systematic and definitive listing of traditions of gameday weekends, nor is it a detailed and exhaustive history of such traditions. It is instead a snapshot of traditions and connections that the authors found compelling during their explorations of gameday weekends during the 2005, 2006, and 2007 seasons. It was in this way, engaged with the individuals who make the gameday experience so rich, that the broad-reaching connections between diverse communities stirred our curiosity and invited fans' further exploration. It is our hope that you will enjoy this book, and come to appreciate the depth of what gameday means to Notre Dame fans of every sort.

1

WE ARE ND

The Students as Stars and Supporters

Football weekends are the times when company is coming—on a grand scale—and students see good things to preserve and put on display. Many of them have grown up in families that are highly engaged in the social, cultural, business, and professional worlds. As members of the so-called millennial generation, they value being well connected, tuned in, and part of things that are much bigger than themselves. But they're also eager to exhibit the deeper story about their own roles as individuals, their own gifts, their own perspectives on the value of the community life they have been privileged to discover. This chapter explores many of the ways students take part in and benefit from involvement with gameday festivities and traditions.

1

Students in the Stadium

The focal point of every gameday weekend is of course the football game itself. The stadium provides a central location for the students to gather and make connections—with each other and with broader communities.

Head football coach Charlie Weis '78 likes to emphasize the connection between the football team and their fellow students in making a game successful. Speaking at the stadium pep rally that preceded the 2006 home opener against Penn State, he said he had modified his earlier thinking that the team had to disengage a bit from the emotions of a home game in order to maintain their focus. This time, he said, "I've really encouraged our football team to embrace this whole event, to get ready for Penn State as being part of it, not as our own separate entity."

But that coin has two sides, Weis continued. "We want *you* to be a part of this game," he told the students in the stands. "We need your help." Tomorrow, during the game, throughout the game, whenever Penn State is on offense, "you should be very, very *loud*."

The passing along of lessons and traditions among the student body is facilitated by the fact that such a large percentage of the undergraduate population is present in the stadium for every game, every year, says Cappy Gagnon '66, who is manager of event security for the Notre Dame Security Police and coordinator of stadium personnel for the athletics department. Indeed, this critical mass of students allows the students themselves to be the creators and stewards of traditions. In the stadiums of many universities, only a relatively small percentage of the student body is present, leaving the bulk of a game's energy in the hands of fans who, while they are loyal and valued supporters, bring a more casual than collectivist mentality. "Fans are a little different than *tradition guardians*," says Gagnon.

That's not all. The Catholic culture at Notre Dame fosters a respect for tradition and group engagement in ritual. In addition, the fact that roughly a quarter of the students present at Notre Dame have been legacy students, with an inbred investment in the traditions, adds even more to the sense of stewardship, Gagnon points out. Also conducive to the preservation and nurturing of traditions is the sense of connection that comes from these students' shared experiences, taking many of the same courses in their first year and facing together the rigors of a Notre Dame education. In short, Notre Dame is all about participation.

The Band Plays On

"The Band of the Fighting Irish" is one of the focal points of attention on gameday weekends. They too have stories to tell of their long, proud history, the extraordinary energy of their

preparation and performances, a panoply of traditions, and their close integration with the spirit of Notre Dame football. This group of 380 students constitutes the oldest university band in continuous existence in the country. It is known to have existed in 1846, just four years after Rev. Edward Sorin, CSC, and his colleagues founded the school. It has been declared a "Landmark of American Music."

Under the leadership of Director of Bands Dr. Kenneth Dye, the band practices every day, totaling about nine hours between Monday evening and Saturday morning, for an upcoming home game. "We do a brand new show for every home game," says assistant director Larry Dwyer '66, and that demands learning new music as well as new formations—most of the latter designed by assistant director Sam Sanchez. A typical half-time show consists of three songs plus, of course, the "Notre Dame Victory March," a song that marks its one-hundredth anniversary in 2008. Townspeople have a chance to see and hear the latest routines when the band holds its Friday af-

ternoon practice in the parking lot north of Edison Road near Eddy Street.

But halftime pageantry is only part of the band's role. After having completed an hour of gameday practice on the indoor field of Loftus Center, they present their Saturday concert for fans on the steps of Bond Hall, the School of Architecture's headquarters. The venue for this concert was moved from the steps of the Golden Dome years ago when the Main Building was

being renovated. The move had side benefits, such as protection of the God Quad's flowerbeds from the crowds of listeners. Most importantly, this band, growing from its earlier size of about 125 (all male) players, could no longer be contained by the Main Building's staircase.

The band continues to demonstrate its fierce energy as it marches briskly from the Golden Dome to the stadium, led by the Irish Guard, accompanied by cheerleaders, and cheered on by thousands of fans who line the parade route. Soon, it pours out onto the field to spell out the word "Irish" and to begin the pregame ritual of playing "America the Beautiful" and "The Star-Spangled Banner." The music beautifully reflects the University's motto, "God, Country, Notre Dame." In the stadium, one of the great traditions is that people actually sing both songs.

Another aspect of that spirit is the band's hospitality. It plays the school song of the visiting team during pregame festivities. The director of the visiting band is invited to lead Notre Dame's musicians in "The Star Spangled Banner." There are some games, however, when that director had better get on with it: at games when there is a fly-over by military jets, split-second timing is required to allow for the roar of their passage to perfectly punctuate the end of the anthem. By the way, the hospitality continues after the game as Notre Dame's band invites the opposing team's musicians to a modest reception and often gives the visiting band's director a memento. Visiting teams love to bring their bands to Notre Dame to share in the special experience of a football game in Notre Dame stadium. By the time the visiting band joins in a reception at the Ricci Band Rehearsal Hall, Notre Dame's musicians have marched approximately seven miles.

The Band: We Are ND

Giant state universities might have no trouble fielding a marching band with hundreds of mem-

bers, but Notre Dame's smaller size means that a higher proportion of the student body is in the Band of the Fighting Irish. Moreover, all these students join the band because they want to— as distinct from the practices of some universities that require their music majors (from their large schools of music) to play in the band, perhaps for a year or two. In fact, Notre Dame has relatively few music majors; there were fewer than ten of them in the band during the 2006 season. And almost all members stay in the band all four years. It really is a representative student band.

> The Notre Dame band's website (ndband.com) reports that legendary Fighting Irish coach Knute Rockne was a flute player in Notre Dame's concert band.

The Music Takes Over

A band with 380 members necessarily stresses its suborganization into instrumental units, which wind up having their own identities and traditions. "Each section functions as a tight-knit group," says Dwyer. "They develop their own styles and ways of doing things." Various instrumental sections have their own distinct traditions.

For example, the Drummer's Circle brings a special kind of energy to their performances. Among their most energetic and tradition-rich performances is their appearance at midnight in front of the Main Building every Friday before a home game. With hundreds of undergraduates already assembled on the building's steps and porch, the crowd moves aside for, and then encircles, the drummers. These musicians then pro-

ceed to stir up their fellow students with thunderous riffs and routines that constitute the kind of pseudo-tribal cheering practice that would thrill a professor of anthropology.

Earlier on Fridays, the trumpet section makes its ritual appearance around the Main Building's rotunda at 4:00 pm. Its blaring call to arms symbolically starts the football weekend for hundreds of fans and includes both the Victory March and the Alma Mater. They then join the entire band outside the Main Building, and the entire troop marches across campus toward its Friday rehearsal.

The trumpet section also has other traditions, reports student trumpeter Charlie Vogelheim '09. After the Saturday morning "concert on the steps" at Bond Hall, the band disperses for a brief time, and various sections enact their own pregame traditions. The trumpet section again plays the Alma Mater in the rotunda of the Main Building. Everyone gathers again outside the Main Building and Washington Hall (where the band used to be housed). From there, the band fires up for its march to the stadium. During the game, when the band plays the Victory March after touchdowns, the trumpets perform a routine wherein they swing into different directions and positions every couple of beats. This is called "Vogue Trumpets," a reference to a hit song by Madonna that calls on the listener to "strike a pose." At the 2006 Sugar Bowl, Vogelheim reports, the trumpeters present in New Orleans couldn't play under the Dome of the Main Building, but they played in the lobby of their hotel.

Serious Stepping

Another section of the band with its own strong identity and tradition is the Irish Guard, the group of ten tall, kilt-wearing soldiers of song who clear the way for the band to march. They also participate in the band's other activities and halftime performances, as well as the flag presentation before each game. Their imposing group was established in 1949, according to the band's website. A story by Beth Erickson in the *Observer,* the campus newspaper, states that their distinctive tartan plaid kilts, adopted in the 1970s, are officially known as "Notre Dame plaid." The design, certified as Irish, not Scottish, is registered in Edinburgh, Scotland.

The Guards must be at least 6'2" in height, with an outstanding stature and style while marching, as well as an ability to transform that

march into a Victory Clog. The clog, performed to the school song "Damhsa Bua," written by former band director Robert F. O'Brien, may be observed a few times on gameday weekends, hopefully including when the game ends in a Notre Dame victory. They must be stone-faced when in uniform. And, until 2000, it appeared they must be men.

But that was one of those traditions just waiting to be broken. Molly Kinder became the first woman Irish Guard in 2000, confronting with courage and good spirit the occasional tensions of being a pioneer. In 2006, junior Tess Murray, a former instrumentalist with the band, became the second woman Irish Guard after she emerged from competition with nearly three dozen aspirants. "In my opinion and in the opinion of the Guard, I am no different than any of them,"

Molly Kinder, the first woman in the Irish Guard, went on to do graduate study in global health at Harvard University, participating in a program created by Jeffrey Sachs. This economist, director of the UN Millennium Project, was one of the panelists for the second annual Notre Dame Forum, held on September 14, 2006. The forum, titled "The Global Health Crisis: Forging Solutions, Effecting Change," captured the imaginations of many students and others in the Notre Dame community, and it led to the establishment of the Notre Dame Millennial Development Initiative in Uganda. The initiative taps into areas of knowledge that can encourage advances in communities' agriculture, education, and health. Kinder herself has written about these sources of hope for sustainable development as co-author of the 2004 book, *Millions Saved: Proven Successes in Global Health*.

Murray was quoted as saying in the *Observer*. "I don't want to be the only one singled out . . . it's not fair to anyone on the Guard."

Adhering to another tradition prior to the first home game of the season, the 2006 team of Irish Guards underwent inspection by alumni who had been members of the unit. In a proud sign of solidarity, Molly Kinder was among those conducting the inspection and finding their successors fit for duty.

Cheer, Cheer for Old Notre Dame

Cheerleaders also have an intensely busy weekend when the Fighting Irish are playing at home.

It actually starts on Friday before the game, when they make a four o'clock appearance at the bookstore and perform some cheers. Then it's off to the Joyce Center, where they join the band and the pom squad at the pep rally, bursting into the arena to the sound of the Victory March. After the rally, cheerleaders may attend other community gatherings to greet visiting team fans and corporate sponsors.

On gameday, four hours before kickoff, the group of six couples assembles in full uniform—including gold shamrock earrings for the women—to go anywhere the echoes could use some waking up. Accompanied by the leprechaun, who is one of them, they visit the Hammes bookstore, Legends, and the Joyce Center. "It's about being with the fans," says Brooke Mohr, one of the senior cheerleaders in 2006. "No one else puts themselves out there" for such extensive and intensive fan contact, she says proudly.

After a warm-up in the stadium, they run to and through key pregame gathering sites, including visits to the Monogram Room and corporate tents. They grab a bite to refuel at their coach's office before their run through various parts of campus, high-fiving with the crowd, on their way to an eventual rendezvous with the band to march across campus and into the stadium.

Before that rendezvous, they gather for a moment of relative quiet at the Nieuwland Science Building. The leprechaun summons them to

prayer—the Hail Mary—followed by a cry of "Go Irish," after which they storm through LaFortune Student Center on their way to the Dome in time for the band's step-off.

The parade to the stadium passes by spots of personal importance to the cheerleaders—one place where their parents traditionally assemble and another where cheerleader alumni offer their own support. As everyone approaches the stadium, the cheer is, "Here come the Irish." After their entry onto the field, as the band is playing, they do a long cheer with kicks—named the Rally—"that's been passed down forever," says Mohr.

They high-five the Notre Dame football players storming onto the field, having been noticeably silent while the opposing team entered. During the game, the senior cheerleaders, called the "gold squad," stoke the flames of spirit in the student section. A favorite cheer in the fourth quarter is "We are ND," as the four corners of the stadium echo with school spirit.

In 2005, a second squad of six additional couples began cheering at the south end zone of the stadium. These are sometimes the same students who will also cheer at a soccer game on Sunday, making for a very busy weekend.

"Goodwill ambassadors of our great university is a good description of a Notre Dame cheerleader," says Jonette Minton, who has coached the cheerleaders for more than a dozen years. "The interaction with the community at home and, while on road trips, with our teams is what it's all about."

A Special Group

Is it corny or immature to be cheering with the spirit that imbues Notre Dame students at a football game? Brooke Mohr comments that sometimes rival teams' fans—or even their cheerleaders—raise the question, at least implicitly, Who do you think you are?

"Notre Dame incites something in you, no matter who you are, to just be happy with who you are and where you are and being surrounded by good people. It's a feeling you're not going to have unless you come here," says Mohr.

The competition to join the cheerleaders is intense, starting at the end of the first year of studies. Out of fifty to sixty students trying out, only a half dozen or so can be admitted into the beginner squad. Like so many other student activities, cheerleading becomes a cornerstone of friendship and shared effort, even among people who have grown up wanting to be on top. "Everyone's very competitive," says Mohr, "so it's great being able to work together."

One of Mohr's best cheerleading memories has nothing to do with football. She and her colleagues arrive a week before the start of the academic year, partly so they can practice for the pep rally that is a centerpiece of Frosh-O, the orientation weekend for first-year students. "It's so neat to be part of the freshman pep rally. You look into the crowd, and everyone is so enthralled by what you're doing and the fact that you're representing Notre Dame." Cheerleading is less a show than an interaction, almost a dialogue, almost a gift of self. "We're definitely a part of bringing the freshmen in," says Mohr. "You're creating community for everyone."

Minton feels a special familial tie to the cheerleading program and to each year's group. "At the year-end banquet, I often say I don't think we can top this year's team—and then each year I find myself being truly amazed that they do," she says. "The students are great, and I love them."

There Be Leprechauns Here

The leprechaun is a natural mascot for a team called the Fighting Irish. Although the famous cartoon logo features a leprechaun ready for a fight, the aggressiveness of the live mascot is limited to the enthusiasm with which he leads cheers and greets gameday attendees. The friendliness and hospitality of the leprechaun is so important that, during parts of gameday, a sort of "leprechaun escort" is on duty to help keep him—and the cheerleading squad that accompanies him—on schedule and undeterred by people whose requests for photos and other wishes might not be possible to grant.

The leprechaun you'll see on gameday is part of the cheerleaders' "gold squad." He had to work hard for that position. During the spring semester, there is a week-long process of clinics and competitions. The pool of aspiring leprechauns is trimmed down as they demonstrate their physical fitness, creativity, and charisma in front of crowds, their poise in media settings, and their spirit for representing Notre Dame. Some of the sorting-out process takes place in competitions to which the student body is invited and during which students root for their dorm mates or other favorites. Judges include cheerleading coach Jonette Minton and representatives of the athletics department, athletics promotions, student activities office, alumni office, academic services office, and former leprechauns—preserving continuity with the past. This group also interviews the candidates individually.

Leprechauns have been the official mascot since the 1960s. Some time before that, the mascot role was filled by Irish terriers, usually called Clashmore Mike.

Kevin Braun, a red-headed computer science major from Pennsylvania, was the gold squad leprechaun for the 2006 season. In spring 2007, senior Braun handed on the job to junior Matt Phipps. The "blue squad" of cheerleaders has its own leprechaun. For the 2006–07 academic year, that was Juan Muldoon, Notre Dame's first Mexican leprechaun. Muldoon earned the blue squad title again for the 2007 season. Notre Dame's first African-American leprechaun, Michael Brown, led the cheers in 1999–2000. He has since been elected to represent young alumni on the board of directors of the Notre Dame Alumni Association.

There's a Party Going On

The Friday evening pep rally that precedes Saturday home games is a long-standing tradition that has gone through some metamorphosis, expert observers say. Its current venue, in the Joyce Center, allows for a good show that includes brief talks by Coach Charlie Weis and

The pom squad is a group of female dancers, separate from the cheerleaders and functioning as a club under the auspices of Student Activities. They do not go on the field during football games, although they perform on Saturday for the fans in the Joyce Center, and they also entertain at basketball games.

some of his players, plus plenty of stimulation from the leprechaun, the cheerleaders, the band, the alumni, and the pom squad.

Pep rallies in their former, smaller venues of past decades, the Old Fieldhouse and then the Stepan Center, are said to have been rougher around the edges and less likely to be enjoyed—or seen— by visitors from off-campus and tourists with children. For one thing, the former venues required that most people stand—quite compactly.

Some members of the Notre Dame family are nostalgic for the old emphasis on emotional buildup as opposed to the new emphasis that puts team support in a broader context of sharing history and anticipation, enjoying entertainment, welcoming players from the past, showing student solidarity, and

offering open arms to the broader community. Nevertheless, students still embrace today's rallies as a chance to burn off (and kindle) their energy en masse, letting loose with song and dance and high-decibel cheering. By somewhat recent tradition, each pep rally is sponsored by several designated residence halls. Those students get the best seats in the front rows and add their own distinctive gestures and messages to the hoopla.

It should be noted that Dillon Hall ranks first, at least chronologically, in its pep rally leadership. By tradition, that dorm holds its own first rally of the season—on the Thursday night before the first game. But of course other residence halls find numerous ways to participate in the excitement all season long—by hanging banners out of windows and waking up their freshman members, and their neighbors, on the year's first gameday with a five am sing-along, for example.

Students may be dressed in all sorts of garb, and they might take a detour at any hour through the Clarke Memorial fountain. The dorms see to it that the edgy, homemade excitement that may have been epitomized in the Stepan Center is still alive among the students.

The most radical departures from the Stepan Center rallies of the past have been occasional decisions to place the Friday evening event in the stadium itself. Such rallies are great chances to bring even more students together and to invite large numbers of townspeople and visitors to experience the stadium's magnificence (and the student body's spirit) without buying a game ticket.

Among the approximately 200 recipients of honorary monograms are former Presidents Gerald Ford and Ronald Reagan, Pope John Paul II, Notre Dame President Emeritus Rev. Theodore M. Hesburgh, CSC, and former Irish football coaches Ara Parseghian and Lou Holtz.

Notre Dame's embrace of tradition and its celebration of connections were in the spotlight during the stadium pep rally before the Sept. 9, 2006, game against Penn State. Monogram Club president Julie Doyle, executive director Jim Fraleigh, Monogram winner Dr. Dennis Nigro, and former College Football Hall of Fame executive director Bernie Kish joined in presenting an honorary monogram to Easter Heathman. Easter was saluted as the unofficial caretaker of the site near Bazaar, Kansas, where legendary coach Knute Rockne died in a plane crash on March 31, 1931. Easter, a local resident then age 13, arrived at the site with his mother and father shortly after the crash. Later in life, he devoted much energy to preserving the memory of Rockne, organizing tours of the site and memorial ceremonies.

Also during that pep rally, Coach Weis announced the start of a new tradition: the team joining the student section at the end of every home game to sing together the Alma Mater. Weis explained that he had gotten the idea immediately after the 2005 game against Navy, when he saw that team join their fellow students and fans to proudly sing their alma mater. Why don't we do that? Weis thought. "So tomorrow starts a new tradition at Notre Dame."

Do I Hear Bagpipes?

The Notre Dame Bagpipe Band, as a student club, has a somewhat less "official" standing among

the activities of gameday, but it has a proud tradition connected to football revelry. It also represents a connection to the Notre Dame faculty and the South Bend community.

The Irish Guard began their existence in 1949 as the bagpipe unit of the Notre Dame band. They learned that bagpipes were not well suited to the cold weather that ensued as the football season progressed, so they abandoned the instruments.

In 1987, a student, Paul Harren '91, resurrected the presence of bagpipes on campus when he decided to form a band. Robert Howland, a bagpiping member of the faculty, became their adviser, and the Student Union Board provided financial support. In 2000, the group achieved a critical mass of experienced bagpipers, and they marched for the first time during the 2001 football season. The Irish Guard generously provided old kilts, and the bagpipers were joined by drummers who played traditional bagpipe beats. They have since been joined by new faculty advisers: first, Dominic Vachon, and then by his successor, Dan Gezelter, a bagpiper and professor of chemistry and biochemistry.

Today's bagpipe band is a talented group of students who wear the traditional Notre Dame tartan plaid worn by the Irish Guard, and they consistently invite Vachon and Gezelter to be part of their marching retinue as well as provide bagpipe instruction. "It's one of the favorite things I do in my life," says Vachon, who now works at St. Joseph Regional Medical Center.

> The Bagpipe Band makes music on occasions other than gameday. They are frequently asked to play in front of the Basilica for weddings, and they have played at memorial services.

These days, another local bagpipes entrusiast has offered help with weekly lessons to freshmen who are new to the bagpipes. "Over half the band consists of students who are starting from scratch," says Michael Kelley '07, who served as club president and pipe major during his senior year.

"The bagpipes tend to evoke an emotional response from people, and it's so satisfying to have that kind of effect," says Kelley. "Whether I'm marching with pipers and drummers before football games or just playing beside the lake at dusk, I like to think that I am contributing to the Notre Dame tradition and adding to the aura of the campus."

The group is indeed a regular presence on gameday, although they are careful not to com-

The Notre Dame Bagpipe Band plays outside the Knights of Columbus building.

pete with the marching band's premier musical role or its Bond Hall concert. The bagpipers perform in front of the Dome and—in tribute to past support offered by the Knights of Columbus—at the site of the Knights' steak sandwich stand. They march through LaFortune Student Center, around the stadium before the game, and are occasionally invited to appear at the Friday pep rallies, at the bookstore, and at particular tailgates.

In 2006, Paul Harren '91, the alumnus who helped to bring bagpipes back to Notre Dame in 1987, showed up in his kilts and performed with the group.

Their crowd-drawing performances at the steak sandwich sale have encouraged the use of that site by other student groups, like jugglers, in a way that reminds Vachon of the bagpipers' own nascent days in the 1990s. "This is the evolution of a tradition," he says.

The bagpipe group itself has continued to grow. It comprised thirteen pipers (including Dominic and Dan) and seven drummers in 2006, the largest contingent yet. An even bigger group geared up to perform in 2007.

Broadcasting the Game

Why should the professional journalists have all the fun of covering the game? Notre Dame football—along with other sports—has long been a training ground for students with a flair for sportswriting and sportscasting. WVFI, the student-run, Internet-only radio station, has been broadcasting the football games since 2000.

WVFI sports director Rok Kopp (right) and sportscaster Brandon Reichardt shared the microphone during a game.

Notre Dame student broadcasters cover virtually all campus athletics throughout the year on the Internet, on the radio station WSND-FM, and on the campus cable television system, NDTV. Even if the students don't need a demo tape for that first media job interview, they can feel especially close to the action while helping others to feel close, too.

Taking a Stand

The attitude of trust and candor that students share with gameday visitors clearly extends to their expression of what's in their hearts, concerns that motivate them all year round as human beings.

In recent years, for example, pro-life students on campus have posted crosses and flags memorializing deaths due to abortion. This display, covering a wide stretch of ground outside the Law School, clearly could not survive the pedestrian traffic of an actual gameday, but it was up on the Friday afternoon before the 2006 Notre Dame-Stanford game as visitors gathered to see the Band's late afternoon march from the Dome to the stadium.

Such displays must always be approved by the Office of Student Affairs. They are one of the many ways in which students are learning to communicate with the outside world on multiple levels, through various media, about many messages, without the kind of one-track think-ing—"this is only about football"—that con-forms to a shallow sound-bite culture and ultimately could lead even to a cheapening of gameday as "just another sporting event."

Showing Guests a Good Time

One of the most important ways in which stu-dents lend a hand in sharing the values and ex-periences that mean a lot to them is service as a tour guide. A number of students provide tours around the Notre Dame campus, satisfying visi-tors' curiosity and opening their eyes to impor-tant aspects of the University's tradition and environment. Football weekends are the busiest time for tours, says veteran guide Kevin Glea-son '08.

Feed Me

Student groups enjoy a golden opportunity to raise money for their own activities when they set up their stands to sell staples like hot dogs, hamburgers, and pop at various spots on campus during the hours before kickoff. The student activities office authorizes about twenty student concession stands for each gameday weekend.

The stands are regulated. For example, if they choose to cook, their grill must be covered by a canopy—just in case any birds were to fly by with the intent of leaving a calling card. Students will also have to show up very early on Saturday morning to get supplies from Food Services.

The best-known and most monetarily successful stakeout sells steak sandwiches made by

Notre Dame's own student council of the Knights of Columbus. Knights Council 1477 says it has been grilling steaks on gamedays for about forty years. The tradition started as a tailgate for council members, but the proximity of the council's headquarters to the former location of the bookstore helped to generate crowds and the idea of raising money for charity through sales to the general public.

During the 2007 season, the Knights say they sold over twenty thousand steak sandwiches at six dollars each and raised over sixty-three thousand dollars, which was donated to roughly thirty charities. The amount for charity was up about 33 percent from the figure for 2005. According to Grand Knight Nathan Menendez, a member of the class of '09, charities receiving at least five thousand dollars included:

Hamburgers may cost you a few dollars, but prayer cards are free. That was the offer when a group of young men discerning their vocation to the Holy Cross priesthood manned this station on gameday and offered holy pictures to passers-by.

- A Holy Cross mission in the Andes Mountains, suggested to the council by Rev. Theodore Hesburgh, CSC.
- A school in Kibera, Africa, founded by a Holy Cross priest, that seeks to help women in the city's slums break the cycle of poverty through education in business and other skills.
- A new program to encourage vocations to the religious life by providing scholarships so other Knights councils in Indiana can send

high school youth to NDVision, the summertime career path discernment camp in which Notre Dame students serve as facilitators.

The Shirt

By far the most successful student-run fund-raiser connected to Notre Dame football is the annual project that designs, produces, and sells "The Shirt." Since the tradition of creating a new shirt each year began in 1990, students have raised more than four million dollars for a select group of student causes. The first shirt, intended to unify the student section in green garb, helped to raise money for the campus's traditional An Tostal spring festivities. Excitement surrounding the 2006 season helped sales of the "Tradition" shirt, designed by senior Ryan Ricketts, to raise more than six hundred thousand dollars, breaking all previous records.

Sister Jean Lenz, OSF, special assistant to the vice president for student affairs, tells the story of how the earliest days of shirt projects quickly reached new charitable heights. In late 1989, a graduate student from China was seriously injured when hit by a car on campus. He spent more than a year in local health-care facilities, and his parents also endured financial and medical challenges after coming to South Bend to be with their son. Urged on by Sister Jean and Joe Cassidy, director of student activities, the various residence hall presidents decided to support a special blue shirt for the eagerly awaited 1990 Notre Dame-Miami game to raise money for the graduate student. The shirt sold very well, both before the game and after Notre Dame's victory, raising money to help pay some of the outstanding bills and to give the family a substantial sum that could be used as they returned to China in 1991, anticipating a round of additional costs adapting their life to the ongoing medical needs of their son.

Nowadays, each year's net revenues go into a few different funds that represent ways in which the students help each other—providing financial support for clubs and organizations, helping students who face extraordinary medical expenses, and building what is called the Rector Fund, says Ryan Willerton, director of student activities facilities. This latter pool of money, overseen by the Office of Student Affairs, helps

Members of the 2007 Shirt student team, from left, Brad LeNoir, Carla DeMarzo-Sanchez, Matt Barloh, Jason Gott, Joyce Almario, display shirts from past seaons.

By 2006, the tradition of "The Shirt" had grown so much that an entire committee of students had to be formed to manage the whole project. Rich Fox served as president for the record-breaking 2006 program. The new committee for 2007 announced plans to spread the tradition nationwide through increased sales to Notre Dame "subway alumni" who might want to express their solidarity at game watches around the country.

students participate in aspects of campus life that they otherwise could not afford (volunteer service trips, class rings, and so on).

The tradition of this "uniform" for fans has been spreading throughout the stadium, with alumni and visitors joining the students in wearing and sharing the spirit of solidarity. "It isn't just a normal t-shirt," comments one student. "It brings everyone together." Another adds: "This shirt represents the service aspect" of the Notre Dame community. Other schools have shirts designed for particular sports, but they are often used only to impart information like the current season and its game schedule, but very few schools appear simultaneously to link a sport to an inspiring message about (and passionate support for) its tradition, to a fund-raising effort for the entire student community, and to the creative work of a team of students who contribute their talents for design, marketing, and salesmanship.

Planning for the 2007 shirt began during the 2006 season when students applied for the position of managing the endeavor. A sophomore, Brad LeNoir, was chosen for the job. This was followed by a design competition and the grand unveiling of the new shirt took place at the

Hammes Notre Dame Bookstore on the eve of the spring 2007 Blue-Gold Game.

Student Managers

One group of students offers its service directly, and indispensably, to the football team. Like the players themselves, the football student managers—primarily twenty-one juniors (along with some sophomores) led by three seniors and overseen by athletics department equipment managers Henry Scroope '97 and Matt Kerls '04—are busy all week long.

The Blue-Gold Game itself is largely intended as a fund-raiser, annually generating hefty amounts for scholarships for students from the Michiana area.

Perhaps the most storied function these students play is the painting of the players' gold helmets. This work, now conducted on Mondays, begins with the stripping and buffing of helmets after they took their beatings on the prior Saturday. Then each helmet gets a basic gold-colored coat of paint, followed by a coat that contains actual particles of gold. For home games, when all of the team members are suited up, the work entails more than one hundred helmets and stretches from mid-afternoon into nighttime, and it's done in the often chilly open-air of the stadium.

Managers stay busy all week. Other preparatory work begins on Monday with the cleaning of cleats and other gear. On Tuesdays through Thursdays, the student managers are with the team for its practices, setting up the field equipment, working in the locker room, and cleaning up. Thursday nights bring more detailed preparation for the upcoming Saturday game. Every player's equipment is moved from the locker room of the Don F. and Flora Guglielmino Athletics Complex locker room to the Stadium locker room. Each locker must be in excellent condition, with everything on hand exactly where it should be, ready for use. This work continues on Friday. For away games, the same

Thursday move of equipment from the Gug entails placement in a truck that will take the supplies to the opponent's stadium. A rotating contingent of about ten student managers—seven juniors and three seniors—accompanies the team to each away game.

Gameday Saturdays mean an early-morning start to the setting-up of team equipment on the Notre Dame Stadium field and sidelines. The managers are on hand to help when the players arrive in the stadium for their early drills. The coaches' headsets are tested. During the game, managers raise and lower the field goal nets, manage the game balls, and keep paperwork important to player statistics and after-game analysis. Work isn't completed until after the game because all the equipment must be brought back to the Gug—a task that stretches well into the evening.

It's a busy week, but "I would never trade it for anything," says junior football manager Anna Jordan. "I can say I worked for the Notre Dame

The state-of-the-art Guglielmino Athletics Complex opened in 2005 as headquarters for the football program but is also used by other student athletes for team meetings, sports medicine, and exercise and training. It is nicknamed the Gug, pronounced "goog."

football team." What's more, each of the twenty-one football managers earns a varsity letter for their work and time commitment to the football team.

The junior football managers rank their own performance as well as that of their colleagues, and these rankings help to determine who will become the three senior football managers and the senior managers for each of the other Notre Dame varsity teams. Rankings also help to determine whether a given senior manager earns a cash award in compensation. Such assistance is not provided in the first three years.

The unpaid work is long and hard, but it typically doesn't deter some one hundred and fifty

first-year students from signing up for student manager work. By the time they return as sophomores, some eighty students may remain on duty after the preliminary tastes they received as freshmen, and these sophomores will be assigned to the various varsity teams, with occasional assignments to help out at the home football games. Their self-ranking will result in the selection of twenty-one junior managers for football. The ranking is gender-neutral; in 2006, there were thirteen women and eight men, but those numbers were reversed in 2005, says Anna Jordan.

The managers have their own traditions, including their own football game on the practice fields, with juniors and seniors privileged to suit up in the game uniforms that they have been caring for all season. A female managers' flag football game has recently been added to the longer-running match between male managers.

Taken to Excess

The momentum of excitement and camaraderie that builds up on a gameday weekend is not without its danger of excess. The virtuous call to "moderation in all things" is consistently forgotten by a few students, as well as other fans and visitors, especially when it comes to partying. For the student community, the chief enforcer of that call to virtue is William Kirk, associate vice president for residence life in the Office of Student Affairs.

Kirk has had this difficult job for nearly two decades. When he arrived on the scene, he had his work cut out for him: an informal infrastructure of some negative traditions had grown up around home games to encourage excess in alcohol use among those so inclined. In a parking area called Gold Field, recreational vehicles had started appearing as early as the Tuesday before a home game, facilitating long bouts of partying in one or two lots. "The place became not an academic institution, but a campground," Kirk recalls.

Things changed bit-by-bit. The stadium became an alcohol-free zone. Fans were prohibited from leaving the stadium at halftime and returning. Close-in lots were closed to RVs, which were not allowed to park overnight. Preapproval was required for student tailgates. The tailgate parties themselves had to shut down during the game. The police presence was stepped up, with more enforcement against underage drinking and outrageous behavior. Groups of police officers, including the state excise police, cruised parking lots to maintain family-friendly conditions. Officers provide a "ministry of presence—one that we hope encourages students and others to make wise choices about their behavior," says Notre Dame Security Police Director Phillip Johnson.

Each game still has its share of arrests, detentions, and other run-ins with law enforcement officials and ushers. The challenge of keeping a lid on the most unruly behaviors has been constant. It is especially daunting when larger than normal crowds gather for the occasional "games of the century."

"It gets discouraging" sometimes to see the time, energy, and money that must be spent to ensure order, Kirk acknowledges, and especially to see students making bad decisions and suffering the ramifications. But it's necessary to ensure a good experience for the vast majority of people who come to enjoy, and contribute to, a great experience on a grand scale.

All in all, Notre Dame is closer to achieving its goal of maximum hospitality, safety, and civil behavior on gameday. "We're trying to make it more family-friendly," Kirk says. "It's much better than it was." And he's realistic about college students being college students, especially at a major event that can bring out the best and the worst in people. "Well, they're not all saints, but I sure wouldn't call them all sinners either."

Spillover Effects: Fellow Athletes

Student athletes from Notre Dame's twenty-five other sports teams got a chance in 2006 to share in the glory of eighty thousand cheering fans. By tradition, teams in the spring sports were typically introduced on the field during football games as a way to honor their performances from the previous semester. But during the 2006 football season, it seemed natural to extend the introductions—and the applause—to teams from both of the preceding semesters.

Why? The fall and spring season teams together had contributed to make 2005–06 the most successful across-the-board athletic year in Notre Dame history. Nine Notre Dame teams finished in the national top ten in end-of-season rankings, and six sports achieved top ten finishes in NCAA competition. The Irish produced three national coaches of the year: Charlie Weis in football, Tracy Coyne in women's lacrosse, and Jay Louderback in women's tennis. Four programs finished in the top four of their respective NCAA championships: men's and women's fencing (they compete for a combined championship), women's lacrosse, and men's cross country. Notre Dame finished a best-ever sixth in the 2005–06 United States Sports Academy Division

The baseball team takes the field at the 2006 Stanford game.

I Director's Cup all-sports competition, sponsored by the National Association of Collegiate Directors of Athletics.

The spillover effects from Notre Dame football games for other Notre Dame sports and their student athletes are not limited to the applause they receive in the stadium. Football weekends are also the weekends when soccer, volleyball, and other teams have their own competitions scheduled and can draw a large crowd of fans to see their own efforts.

Spillover Effects: Interhall Football

There's another way in which large numbers of Notre Dame students share in the football fever inspired by their varsity team. The residence hall structure at Notre Dame facilitates a very active intramural, or interhall, season of football contests. The men's halls and women's halls have their own competitions, in football and in many other sports.

Fittingly, the interhall football championship games are played in Notre Dame Stadium on the Sunday after the last home game.

Intramural football games, in full pads, are played on Riehle Field near the Stepan Center.

2 PILGRIMAGE

The Spiritual Dimension

Celebrations of faith and football have gone together at Notre Dame for as long as anyone can remember. Although there must be a multitude of prayerful requests for the success of the football team, the connections between faith and gameday on the Notre Dame campus run deeper than that. For many visitors, for example, a gameday weekend invariably includes a visit to the Grotto of Our Lady of Lourdes and the Basilica of the Sacred Heart. But a number of traditions signal aspects of faith that permeate Notre Dame.

Mass for the Masses

The Mass is nearly omnipresent on a gameday weekend. Not counting the customary Sunday

Masses held in each of the twenty-seven (soon to be twenty-eight) residence hall chapels, the Mass schedule as printed in the "Gridiron Graffiti" guide provided to visitors lists about twenty opportunities from Friday through Sunday, including a Mass in Spanish. Fans at Notre Dame Stadium will even receive a Mass reminder during the game.

This supply of liturgies responds to a hunger that apparently has existed for a long time. A former chaplain for the athletics department tells the decades-old story—at least traced from the time when Catholics typically received the Eucharist while kneeling at the communion rail—of an old-timer present for the game. He approached a priest-rector to inquire when his residence hall would hold its Saturday morning Mass. Informed that there was no Mass imminent, he asked, "Where can I go to hit the rail for the boys?"

Mass Appeal

The Basilica of the Sacred Heart welcomes fans to Mass thirty minutes after every home game. But that's not the only place on campus where a Saturday night vigil Mass is attended by fans who got the subtle reminder of their Sunday obligation from an announcement during the game. Overflow crowds join the congregation at Stepan Center, or in numerous residence halls, and there's also a Mass in the Jordan Auditorium of the Mendoza College of Business.

University President Emeritus Rev. Edward A. Malloy, CSC, writes about the Mass phenomenon in his book, *Monk's Notre Dame.* "The mood in the postgame chapels is obviously affected by the outcome of the game, but I have found that

even when Notre Dame loses, everything is put into perspective when one attends Mass so soon after the contest is over. When collections are taken up for some charitable cause, such as the Center for the Homeless or one of the Holy Cross missions, people tend to be quite generous."

Malloy continues his reflection on the Masses of gameday. "One of the great signs of the influence that Notre Dame has had on its graduates is to see them coming back to Mass in the dorms with their own children. There is something so fundamental about common worship in the Notre Dame experience that our grads want to share it with the next generation. I hope and pray that one of the biggest problems on home football weekends will continue to be whether people can find a Mass where they can make it inside, no less find a seat."

Grotto and Basilica

For many gameday visitors, a trip to Notre Dame would be incomplete without stopping for a quick (or not so quick) dip into the pool of prayerfulness.

Notre Dame's replica of the Lourdes grotto where the Virgin Mary appeared to the peasant girl Bernadette Soubirous was built in 1896. There always seems to be someone—and there is often a crowd, miraculously quiet and respectful—visiting this uniquely uplifting spot where prayers sprout like flames from the many burning candles. It builds its own sense of community even as it transports people to a different time and space. The Rosary is prayed every evening at the site.

A visit on the crisply cold Friday night before the last home game of the 2006 season revealed a steady stream of visitors of all ages coming and going, usually after spending a reflective moment on the kneelers or benches. But one group lingered for quite a while, watching a different but related display of love. An undergraduate had set up his own display of lit candles on the ground, arranged to spell out "Will you marry me?" He and some friends awaited the arrival of his girlfriend, happy to share this time of expectancy with unknown tourists and with Mary.

One of the grotto's traditions is that Notre Dame seniors for whom graduation day is imminent make a final visit together as a class to seal their remembrance of connection with each other and with the patroness of their university.

Nearby, a sculpture commemorates Tom Dooley, a Domer from the class of 1948 who became a doctor devoted to caring for the impoverished in Asia and elsewhere. "How I long for the Grotto," he said in a 1960 letter from his faraway deathbed to then-president Rev. Theodore Hesburgh, CSC. A replica of the letter is on display there. Many pause to read it. For some, it has galvanized convictions or inspired careers.

The Basilica offers another inspiring place where visitors escape from the home-game hubbub and immerse themselves in sacred things—grand items of gold and marble, historic treasures of local memory and international religious significance, and settings of quiet awe under and amidst beautiful art. It's a busy place on a gameday weekend—actually, on just about any weekend, as befits a basilica. But the crowds and extra attention drawn to Masses by football weekends

give an opportunity for the University's choirs and instrumentalists to share their enthusiasm more widely.

Prayer Sandwich

The work of communicating the connections between faith and football has been passed down through the decades, largely through the work of the team's chaplains. A number of Holy Cross priests have played this role.

The chaplain whose work is immortalized in the film "Rudy," through his cameo appearance praying the Hail Mary with the team, is Rev. James Riehle, CSC, '49. His spiritual leadership of the football team began in 1966 and extended into the new millennium.

Every Notre Dame football game is bracketed and infused by prayer. On Saturday, as the start of a game draws near and the Irish team returns briefly to its locker room after its warm-up on the field, their home game chaplain—now Rev. Paul Doyle, CSC, long-time rector and an important figure in the Notre Dame community's faith life—stands in the hallway blessing each individual.

Even as a retiree, Father Reihle continued to lead the team—and its fans—in prayer, saying an impromptu grace before meals at the Kickoff Luncheons on the Fridays before home games.

With kickoff approaching, the coach addresses his team and, in conclusion, turns to the chaplain. That's the cue for Doyle to lead everyone in the Our Father. Even though this prayer has replaced the Hail Mary, the appeal to the school's patroness continues as the chaplain invokes "Our Lady of Victory" and those around him reply, "Pray for us."

The chaplain continues to be present for the team as they return through the hallway to the locker room at halftime. He blesses them individually, patting them on their shoulder pads.

"This is important to them," says Doyle.

Again, at the end of the game, win or lose, the chaplain is in the locker room. When invited, he leads the team and coaches in the Lord's Prayer once again and invokes "Notre Dame Our Mother," and all shout "Pray for us." After victories, the team closes this ritual by singing the Victory March.

> Coach Ty Willingham first requested that the Hail Mary be replaced by the Our Father, which was better known by the team's non-Catholic players. That new tradition has continued under coach Charlie Weis.

The Team Mass

The Sunday ritual of many Catholic families—gathering together and heading off to Mass—is repeated every gameday by the Notre Dame football team, but on a larger scale.

About three hours before each home game, spectators near the rear of the Main Building can see the Fighting Irish team buses arrive with their police escort. They have spent Friday night off-campus in a hotel to preserve their pregame focus.

The players, accompanied by their coaches, proceed to the back of the Basilica of the Sacred Heart. (Decades ago, the team Mass was celebrated in a residence hall chapel.) As the players enter the Basilica through the "God, Country, Notre Dame" doorway, commemorating alumni who served in World War I, Father Doyle prepares to celebrate Mass. The setting is the Lady Chapel, a beautiful portion of the Basilica behind the main altar where they are separated from the hubbub of other Basilica visitors and

where ushers keep away all those who are not part of the team.

At the point in the Mass where Catholics believe they are consuming Christ's body and blood under the form of bread and wine, non-Catholic team members join in the procession to the altar and receive a blessing from Father Doyle. The Mass traditionally concludes with veneration of a relic of the True Cross. Since 1923, Notre Dame has possessed a reliquary containing what the Vatican attests to be splinters from the cross upon which Jesus died. It is presented for veneration if the player wishes. The cross holds profound meaning for Catholics and many non-Catholics alike, Father Doyle notes.

The Mass is a special and private time of bonding for the team before it begins its day of battle and brouhaha. Since all Notre Dame residence halls have chapels where students (including many non-Catholics) attend Masses on weekends—and some on weekdays, as well—the Mass is also a familiar comfort zone that makes the connection back to the entire Notre Dame community.

Every Player a Medal Winner

Each team Mass has also traditionally included the blessing and distribution of a medal honoring a particular saint. The medals are intended not as "good luck charms" but as reminders of one of the communities with which the team members—and all Christians—are invited to interact, namely, the communion of saints. Players receive these medals as they exit the Basilica. They might use them to welcome the saint's symbolic presence during the game and might later collect them or share them with girlfriends, says Father Doyle.

The saints represented by the medals are chosen by chaplains for home and away games. They are careful not to repeat the same saint during a five-year period so that no player—even a fifth-year senior—will get the same saint twice. Each medal comes with a lesson—a quick story about something in each saint's life that is worthy of emulating.

Another source of pregame inspiration for the players can come from the homily, which, like the medal, is always part of the team Mass, whether it is home at the Lady Chapel or away in the hotel where the players are staying as the visiting team. A chaplain tries to use his brief homily to tie the day's scripture readings to the game that they're playing, to what team members do, and what students do in life. It all has to be integrated in one's life, a chaplain instructs "and whatever you do, you do it with intensity and passion and to the best of your ability."

After the homily, one chaplain said, the general intercessions always include "that both teams play to the best of their ability, that no one gets hurt, and always thanksgiving for the people who came before us who have led us to this point, our parents, our family, our teachers, our coaches."

Communion is followed by the Litany of the Blessed Mother. After the Mass ends with "Go in peace to love and to serve the Lord," there's one more intercession: "Go Irish."

An away game gives the chaplain a chance to carry the distribution of medals to an extra level of evangelization. He often has carried with him some medals whose two sides honor the guardian angels and St. Michael the Archangel. They play defense in the communion of saints, you might say. He gives these medals in gratitude to the police escorting the team.

A Spirit That Transcends Religions

Immediately before games start, a number of Notre Dame players have been observed kneeling prayerfully in the end zone. This is a powerful testimony to a faithfulness that transcends any particular religion. One of the players observed in that posture was senior offensive lineman Bobby Morton, who served as player representative to the football team's unit of the Fellowship of Christian Athletes (FCA).

The nationwide ministry, which embraces Christians of many denominations, has been welcomed by coach Charlie Weis (and by coach Tyrone Willingham before him), and it counted some twenty players and coaches as members in 2006, according to *Sharing the Victory,* the FCA magazine. "FCA has provided an environment in which we can find the foundation of our beliefs and faith and spread the Word of God through our fellowship," senior quarterback Brady Quinn—a member of the group—was quoted as saying.

Morton suffered the loss of his father to stomach cancer eleven days before the 2006 season opener, but he turned it into a recommitment of faith in the Lord. "I want people to look at Notre Dame football like I did when I was 4," he was quoted as saying in the magazine. "I saw them never give up, but I never heard why. Now, when people ask, 'Why did you go for that ball? Why did you make that tackle? Why did you continue to play hard?' I can say, 'Because I have hope— hope because Christ died for me.' "

The stories of interfaith fellowship on the football team go on. Senior offensive tackle Ryan Harris, a practicing Muslim, gave an interview in 2006 to the *South Bend Tribune* in which he praised Notre Dame for doing "a real good job of making sure I was welcomed to the community" as a first-year student. And the comfort zone extends to the team Mass. "At the Masses, I just take time to participate to the extent that I feel comfortable," he was quoted as saying. "And also I reflect on what I believe and reflect on my blessings and opportunities that are coming up in hours at that point."

Bobby Morton kneels in prayer shortly before gametime.

The Champions in Athletics

In his capacity as chaplain to the whole athletics department, a priest knows that his outreach

In the fall of 2007, Notre Dame's Holy Cross community celebrated the beatification of their founder, Father Basil Moreau, CSC. Cornerstones of Moreau's order include a zeal for bringing hope to those whose lives they touch, as well as faith in God's providence, which is inseparable from the suffering—and the salvation—of Christ's cross.

Moreau gave the Congregation of Holy Cross a special patroness—Our Lady of Sorrows—but hardly to the exclusion of Our Lady of Victory. He also gave the order this motto: "Ave Crux Spes Unica—Hail the Cross, Our Only Hope." The message transcends perseverance to embrace compassion, camaraderie, and confidence that God has his best in store for us, even amid sorrows and sacrifice.

The message seems to extend not only to the team but through the team to the entire campus, and, expressed through the hospitality of both the Holy Cross and the broader Notre Dame communities, the message also seems to transcend particular faiths.

includes most of the varsity teams (every team has a Holy Cross priest as a chaplain). Basketball players are also among those who participate in team Masses and receive medals, for example.

The team spirit actually extends to everyone on the department staff, one chaplain points out. "Our custodians and maintenance people take a real pride" in the athletic buildings, which require much hard work for cleanup and upkeep.

The championship attitude seems to be contagious all over campus, the chaplain adds. It's often rephrased by people as "doing it the Notre Dame way"—that is, driving for excellence.

Other Icons and Sacramentals

There's no problem finding a religious experience at Notre Dame on gameday, thanks partly to the many beautiful statues and settings with religious themes. Likewise, it's easy to entertain one's more secular tastes by whimsically imposing football meanings on works of religious art.

The statue of Rev. William C. Corby, CSC, standing outside Corby Hall not far from the lakes, strikes a pose that has prompted the title "Fair Catch Corby." Of course, the meaning of the statue goes much deeper because it captures the moment in 1863 when this brave Civil War chaplain gave general absolution to the Union

Army soldiers comprising the Irish Brigade, just before many of them went off to fight and die in the Battle of Gettysburg. The statue is a twin of one that stands at the Gettysburg historical site, one of only a few non-soldier statues at Gettysburg. Corby was also the third president of Notre Dame.

The statue of Moses outside the Hesburgh Library has won the title "We're Number One" because this giant figure is pointing skyward toward the one God who has given him and his people the Ten Commandments. He's also been known as "First Down Moses."

The most famous of the mixed metaphors combining religious and athletic iconography is the "Touchdown Jesus" title jocularly given by some fans and media personnel to the "Word of

Life" mural adorning the towering south façade of Hesburgh Library.

The Knute Phenomenon

There are some statues and sites that receive respectful visitations on gameday weekends even though they have nothing to do with theology. For example, people enjoy seeing (and touching) the statues of past coaches Frank Leahy and Ara Parseghian, and longtime athletics director Moose Krause. But undoubtedly the most notable of these have to do with Knute Rockne, who has earned a kind of secular sainthood in the hearts of many Irish fans.

The Rockne Memorial athletic center is home to a bronze bust of Knute that has clearly touched many hearts. That is clear from the number of

people who have touched the statue's nose, leaving it a shining silver color. Students have a tradition of touching his nose for good luck before tests, but many gameday visitors simply come to have their photo snapped with this image of the great coach.

Some folks take a longer trip to pay their respects (with varying degrees of conventionality) to Rockne. They visit his simple grave at South Bend's Highland Cemetery. (Alongside lit candles, a beverage, a "Coach" cap, and other tokens may be found decorating the site.) Three graves are lined up in a row—"Father: Knute Rockne," "Mother: Bonnie Rockne," and "Son: William D."

Nearby is a more stately tribute, erected by his native country, Norway. It salutes "A dynamic, innovative leader who captured America's imagination. He was a builder of champions in football and in life."

This isn't the only way in which the city of South Bend participates in saluting Knute. A statue of him stands proudly near the center of downtown, outside the College Football Hall of Fame.

Also, for several months in 2006–07, the Northern Indiana Center for History marked the seventy-fifth anniversary of Rockne's tragic death by hosting a major exhibit of artifacts from his legendary life. The exhibit, "Rockne: Crossing the Last Chalk Line," attracted many visitors during the 2006 gameday weekends. It featured a number of items that had previously been held privately by individuals, including some collectors in South Bend.

It is not inappropriate for Rockne's status as an iconic hero to be discussed in a chapter devoted largely to the Catholicism of Notre Dame. He converted to Catholicism in 1925, being baptized in the Log Chapel in a private ceremony, according to *Notre Dame: 100 Years* (Arthur J. Hope, CSC, University of Notre Dame Press, 1948). That book quotes Rockne himself, as reported in an earlier biography, citing the religious devotion of his players as one of his reasons for adopting the Catholic faith himself. One day before an away game, he couldn't sleep and went downstairs to the hotel lobby around six o'clock in the morning. He witnessed members of his team hurrying out of the hotel to attend Mass, having sacrificed some precious hours of sleep. "I realized for the first time what a powerful ally their religion was to them in their work on the football field," he said.

G. K. Chesterton

The great British author of the early twentieth century, G. K. Chesterton, spent much of the 1930 fall semester as a guest lecturer at Notre Dame, and histories have noted how comfortable he felt—despite being transported to the American Midwest—at a university named for Our Lady. That semester happened to be the time when the new Notre Dame Stadium was opened.

Chesterton, who had converted to Catholicism, also was a man whose writing celebrated the connections between ideas and people, especially the connections that one could see through the eyes of faith. He penned a poem, "The Arena," that powerfully captured the connection between the Lady on the Dome and the contest in the football stadium, a connection transcending time, recalling the past and replacing it, and giving extra meaning to an athletic spectacle that, like all things in Christ, has been made new.

The Arena

Causa Nostrae Laetitiae [Cause of Our Joy]

(Dedicated to the University of Notre Dame, Indiana)

There uprose a golden giant
    On the gilded house of Nero
Even his far-flung flaming shadow and his image swollen large
    Looking down on the dry whirlpool
    Of the round Arena spinning
As a chariot-wheel goes spinning; and the chariots at the charge.

    And the molten monstrous visage
    Saw the pageants, saw the torments,
Down the golden dust undazzled saw the gladiators go,
    Heard the cry in the closed desert
    Te salutant morituri,
As the slaves of doom went stumbling, shuddering,
    to the shades below.

    "Lord of Life, of lyres and laughter,
    Those about to die salute thee,
At thy godlike fancy feeding men with bread and
    beasts with men,
    But for us the Fates point deathward
    In a thousand thumbs thrust downward,
    And the Dog of Hell is roaring through
    the lions in their den."

    I have seen, where a strange country
    Opened its secret plains about me,
One great golden dome stand lonely with its golden image, one
    Seen afar, in strange fulfillment,
    Through the sunlit Indian summer
That Apocalyptic portent that has clothed her with the Sun.

    She too looks on the Arena
    Sees the gladiators grapple,
She whose names are Seven Sorrows and the Cause
    of All Our Joy,
    Sees the pit that stank with slaughter
    Scoured to make the courts of morning

For the cheers of jesting kindred and the scampering
    of a boy.

    "Queen of Death and deadly weeping
      Those about to live salute thee,
  Youth untroubled; youth untutored; hateless war
    and harmless mirth
    And the New Lord's larger largesse
    Holier bread and happier circus,
  Since the Queen of Sevenfold Sorrow has
    brought joy upon the earth."

  Burns above the broad arena
    Where the whirling centuries circle,
Burns the Sun-clothed on the summit, golden-sheeted, golden shod,
    Like a sun-burst on the mountains,
    Like the flames upon the forest
Of the sunbeams of the sword-blades of the Gladiators of God.

    And I saw them shock the whirlwind
      Of the World of dust and dazzle:
  And thrice they stamped, a thunderclap; and thrice
    the sand-wheel swirled;
    And thrice they cried like thunder
    On Our Lady of the Victories,
The Mother of the Master of the Masterers of the World.

    "Queen of Death and Life undying
      Those about to live salute thee;
  Not the crawlers with the cattle; looking
    deathward with the swine,
    But the shout upon the mountains
    Of the men that live for ever
  Who are free of all things living but a Child;
    and He was thine."

                —G.K. Chesterton (1930)

The Alma Mater

The story is told of the discussion in which one person asks another, "Is Notre Dame's Alma Mater a school song or a hymn to
the Virgin Mary?" The other person simply answers, "Yes."

Perhaps because of this dual identity, or because of the many-layered personality of the school that sings it, the Alma Mater is a love song that comes straight from the heart and goes beyond loyalty or tribute. It always seems appropriate, it fits gracefully into nearly any respectful setting, and it is almost never sung as a solo. Indeed, Domers have traditionally made the singing of "Notre Dame, Our Mother" the official completion of their stadium visit on gameday.

Since coach Charlie Weis started the new tradition at the end of the 2006 Penn State game, the team has gathered near the student section and joined their friends and fans in singing the Alma Mater immediately after the game, whether it's a win (sung with pride) or a loss (sung with poignancy). This phenomenon, which has been broadcast over national television, has also proven the song's flexibility—its suitability as a gathering song for true believers or as a closing afterglow broadcast to an international audience.

Both the power and the poignancy are heightened by the story behind the song. By one report, it was written for Knute Rockne's funeral in 1931 and perhaps sung on that occasion by Moreau Seminary members, or it may have debuted at the dedication of Notre Dame Stadium. The words were written by the president of the University, Rev. Charles O'Donnell, CSC, and the music was written by Joseph Casasanta, director of bands and chair of the department of music. According to the Notre Dame Band's website, Casasanta directed the band for nineteen years and composed many school songs for Notre Dame. He did not compose the Notre Dame Victory March, but he wrote an arrangement that the Band still performs.

ECHOES

Alumni, Memories, Gatherings

Some have speculated that the generation of young people now constituting Notre Dame's ranks of undergraduates is poised to be America's next "Greatest Generation," to use the phrase coined by journalist Tom Brokaw in his book about the age cohort that fought World War II. This current generation of "millennials" has been described as desirous of community and heroism, in contrast to autonomy and self-absorption. They value family, with a sense of tradition and responsibility and purposeful accomplishment.

If this is true, there is no better place for millennials than Notre Dame and no better time than gameday. Systematically and spontaneously, students are sharing meaningful life experiences with each other, with their parents, with alumni, and with heroes and legends of the past and present. Alumni are sharing these moments with their children, who are never too young to develop a love for this school and its festival of fellowship. Coaches of all the various Notre Dame varsity teams are sharing these moments with recruits invited in from around the country. This eyewitness experience is the best way for high schoolers to discover the added dimension of alumni loyalty and family sensibilities that they will experience by coming to Notre Dame.

Just as importantly, each generation spends gameday reinforcing its own internal bonds, renewing friendships, and multiplying the quality and quantity of lessons—about love, loyalty, good character, patriotism, fun, faith, and friendship—that it can offer to today's students.

Notre Dame has about 118,000 alumni—nowhere near the number of alumni that much bigger schools can claim. But no school can claim a larger number of loyal alumni who join clubs in their local areas (about 275 clubs, including more than 60 outside the US) and who make the trek from wherever they are to Notre Dame football games, season after season.

Tailgate Fever

While tailgating at many sporting events seems to have become a display of hedonistic and cliquish one-upmanship, tailgating at Notre Dame gamedays continues to be one of the school's most salient trademarks of hospitality and solidarity.

Corporate tents represent the posh component of the tailgating neighborhood—a bit more secluded and selective. They offer their guests, in-

cluding a smattering of celebrities, food delights prepared by Catering by Design, the catering arm of Notre Dame Food Services.

But there continues to be plenty of room for rank-and-file tailgaters, who indulge the notion that anybody can be a celebrity by virtue of experiencing and sharing celebration. They modify the golden rule to say, Celebrate others as you would have them celebrate you. And it works. Sometimes, alumni and guests of the visiting team will set up their own pregame picnic, and they tend to fit right in with the welcoming zeitgeist. But the "mom and pop" tailgates rise like a downtown neighborhood whose loyalties are with Notre Dame.

At times, especially in the lots close to the stadium where many of the tailgaters have been showing up for years—whenever possible, in exactly the same parking spot—it seems less like a collection of individual stakeouts and more like one big party open to all. Hosts at the various stations of food and drink welcome friends and strangers alike, including those wearing the

Notre Dame notables (from left) David Solomon, Ralph McInerny, and William Kirk enjoy tailgating before a game.

opposing team's gear. Equipment includes televisions, heaters, and generators. One pick-up truck was seen serving as a miniature swimming pool. Menus range from hot dogs and beer to shrimp and wine.

Sharing History

If you're an alumnus, there's a table set for you at the Joyce Center fieldhouse where classmates of specific years can mingle at every gameday. Most likely, you've also made your own plans for special reunions and personal rituals, often with game tickets that you've procured as part of your generous giving-back to your alma mater.

Alumni and their kids are among the visitors to the Cyclorama, an exhibit in the fieldhouse that allows you to walk into the middle of a cylindrical panoramic photograph of a game at Notre Dame Stadium. Especially thrilled are the alumni who can find themselves in the photograph.

Some of those alumni not gravitating toward the Joyce Center had established a tradition of visiting the University Club of Notre Dame. The Club, a private and not-for-profit organization with faculty, staff, and alumni members, was founded in 1958. It occupied a building between the Hesburgh Center for International Studies and the McKenna Center. In 2007, the building, with its Rathskeller dining room, Stein Room bar, and Stadium Room for parties, was demolished for construction of a new engineering building.

> Cheerleaders earn a monogram after three years of service with the program, and that honor goes to a leprechaun after two years of service.

On a more official plane, gamedays offer opportunities for the gatherings of various councils and committees of the Alumni Association, Advisory Councils of the various colleges, and even the Board of Trustees. At meetings such as these, discussions of bonds formed in the past are mixed with plans for the future—and for imminent Saturday night social events. Among the groups that assemble are senior alumni, African American alumni, Hispanic alumni, Asian alumni, and Native American alumni. One game is always designated as the "senior game," where Domers who graduated 50 years ago or more are honored. They traditionally have gathered for their own Mass, with Father Hesburgh as celebrant, following the game. The alumni also bestow some of their awards on selected weekends.

The Monogram Club, comprising those alumni and selected honorees who have earned the right to wear Notre Dame's athletic insignia, consciously makes its mission "to bridge the gap between legend and legacy." The club supports not only the physical development of students and alumni, but also their intellectual and spiritual development. The club was instrumental in establishing a Sports Heritage Hall in the Joyce Center, where fans from all backgrounds can find inspiration from sports achievements of the past.

Back with the Band

It's a widespread gameday-weekend tradition for alumni to reunite not only with each other, but with the current students who have taken their places in various teams, clubs, and organizations. When the alumni of the Notre Dame Band do this, it's a reunion of huge proportions— so much so that it happens only once every four years.

Such a reunion took place during the Stanford game in 2006. Indeed, it could only take place during the Stanford game, or another game in which the visiting team is not accompanied by its own band. (That doesn't happen often because visiting bands love to come to Notre Dame Stadium just as much as opposing teams.)

In an event that recalled and topped the grandiose tales of "76 Trombones" told by the fictional Music Man, the Notre Dame Band that day swelled to a population of about thirteen hundred. Nearly nine hundred alumni joined its ranks, says assistant band director Larry Dwyer. When that many people fill the field, they make music "that would bring down the walls of Jericho," he says. The absence of a visiting band helped because, when not performing, all those alumni needed seats.

Honors Across the Board

The Glee Club, which routinely invites its alumni to join in when it performs in the Joyce Center fieldhouse before the games. The sheer numbers and volume don't match the Band, but the enthusiasm and musical joy are equivalent. Peter Mueller is the club's president.

Perhaps the tradition of honoring great athletes in Notre Dame Stadium makes it a place where it is natural to identify and honor the many other people who demonstrate excellence, earn gratitude, and help to represent a kind of collective greatness for a whole community.

The University has taken many opportunities to honor faculty and staff members for significant contributions to Notre Dame as an academic community. Beginning in 2006, for example, Provost Thomas Burish made presentations to outstanding faculty members at the end of the first period. In 2007, the university honored a variety of employees who provide services to students and the whole campus. Troopers from the Indiana State Police, who provide team escorts and traffic assistance, form an impressive line-up on the north end zone during the presentation of the colors.

Flag presentations have been a premier tradition at the beginnings of games. They honor individuals while inviting them to participate in a broader ceremony of pride in community, country, and the virtue of sacrificial service. Participation has been a key, engaging the band, the Reserve Officers' Training Corps (ROTC) color guard, the Irish Guard, the guests of honor, other representatives of the University, and the entire

The 2006 Corby award winner Navy Captain Jack Samar '71 presents the flag to an Irish Guard.

Rex Rakow (right) and his wife Linda at the 2006 flag presentation honoring his service to the university.

stadium to join in a heartfelt rendition of the national anthem. Dennis Brown, assistant vice president for news and information, has been a major force in coordinating flag presentation ceremonies.

One of the flag presentation ceremonies during the 2006 season honored Rex Rakow, long-time director of the Notre Dame Security Police Department who was battling brain cancer. He was accompanied on the field by his wife Linda. Rakow had joined the Notre Dame security staff as assistant director in 1979 and served as director of the Notre Dame Security Police (NDSP)—comprising twenty-nine sworn police officers; forty-seven security officers, monitors, and support staff; and nearly fifty part-time, on-call staff—since 1985. Rakow, a calming and compassionate presence in often stressful circumstances, died on March 7, 2007, and a funeral Mass was celebrated in the Basilica of the Sacred Heart.

The color guard for flag presentations is provided by the ROTC program, in which about three hundred students from Notre Dame, Saint Mary's College, and Holy Cross College are enrolled, according to Lt. Col. Gary Masapollo, former executive officer of the Army ROTC on campus. ROTC also works closely with the Uni-

Football players enter the Sacred Heart Basilica for the team Mass via the "God, County, Notre Dame" entrance.

versity in the planning of other events—such as jet flyovers and jumps into the stadium by the Golden Knights Army parachute team—that honor the military and Notre Dame students' involvement in the armed services through the years. For the Notre Dame–Army game in 2006, Lt. Col. Michael Schellinger '88 coordinated with the Golden Knights to jump in with the official game ball.

The ties between military service and Notre Dame can be traced back far into the University's history. The ROTC program website reports that most Notre Dame students had some sort of military training through the second half of the nineteenth century. In World War I, eight Holy Cross priests enlisted as chaplains, including two who would later become presidents of the university. Students who died in that war are memorialized at the east entrance to the basilica—the entrance that proudly proclaims "God, Country,

Notre Dame." A World War I Army helmet is integrated into the light fixture that you will find overhead immediately upon entering that basilica door.

The presence of a military training program on campus during World War II played no small part in keeping Notre Dame a vibrant educational institution while so many young men were enrolled in the armed services. The Navy established a midshipmen's school, and its V-12 program allowed students to earn commissions in the Navy and Marine Corps while working toward their bachelor's degrees. To this day, respect for the wartime synergy between the Navy and Notre Dame undergirds the tradition of a Notre Dame–Navy football confrontation being scheduled every season.

The Knights of Columbus and "Rudy"

Film still courtesy of TriStar Pictures.

The introduction to Notre Dame (*Spirit of du Lac*) almost always on view at the Eck Visitors Center

isn't the only video entertainment that visitors can catch during gameday. Those who might have stopped by the student council (#1477) of the Knights of Columbus to sample their famous steak sandwiches can duck inside their council headquarters to sit in a comfortable chair and get into the mood by watching the video of *Rudy* that is often playing, free of charge. Grand Knight (for 2007) Nathan Menendez reports that *Rudy* can be rotated with another classic film, *Knute Rockne: All-American*, depending on the vote of the audience at the time. Either way, it's like sitting in a friend's living room and joining them to watch one of their favorite movies.

Planting Seeds in the Next Generation

Keep your eyes open for footballs in flight—not just in the stadium, but all around the campus, on quads and in parking lots, often being thrown by alumni and their kids (and grandkids). It's called quality family time.

Larry Deep and his grandson Brett carry on a Notre Dame tradition by making football their family game.

4 VISITORS

Being Part of Something Big

One key reason for the large gameday attendance that reliably fills Notre Dame Stadium—and includes tens of thousands more people who participate in at least some of the on-campus activities—is the fact that visitors have an enjoyable experience beyond what they would expect from attending the typical football game. It's a given that hospitality "Notre Dame style" requires strength of character, strength of organization, and strength of numbers, but the breadth of what must be done to bring about a successful weekend—for everyone—manifests the need to draw together diverse communities that serve one another.

Surprised by Joy

Gene Russell, an avid Tar Heel fan who attended the 2006 Notre Dame-North Carolina game with his wife, afterwards sent a letter that was reprinted in Notre Dame's faculty-staff newspaper, *ND Works*. "The people of South Bend and specifically the fans and stadium personnel were the most hospitable in the NCAA," he wrote. "We were treated not only as guests but made to feel a part of the Notre Dame tradition. . . . I know we lost [the game] this weekend, but I must tell you we left feeling as if we won."

John "Pepe" Soto, a UCLA alumnus, was quoted in the newspaper as writing this thank-you note to Notre Dame. "We set up our tailgate about 50 yards from the south entrance of the stadium at 8 am. And as we were parking, a man in a Notre Dame ball cap waved us into a slot next to his and said, 'Welcome to Notre Dame!' He was setting up a tailgate too, and he and his friends helped us set up our tent, helped us unload, and then offered us coffee."

The writer went on to say that having UCLA's band director lead the Notre Dame band in the national anthem "was nothing but class." Noting the suspenseful game, he recalled: "At any other college stadium in the country, we would have caught a lot of grief. But at ND, there was nothing but respect for a game well played. Even at our postgame tailgate, ND fans came by to tell us what a great game it was. Some even came with sympathy beers!"

Another memorable commentary was written by *Chattanooga Times-Free Press* journalist Mark Wiedmer in his Nov. 7, 2005, edition after the University of Tennessee suffered a 41-21 defeat in Notre Dame Stadium. "Beneath the pomp and circumstance and century-long run of success,

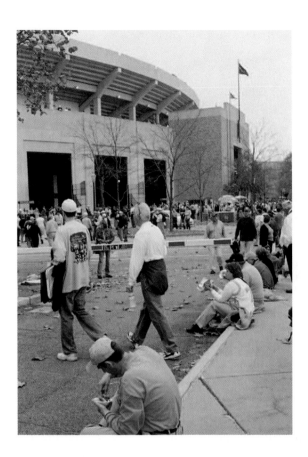

there is a civility and sensibility to Notre Dame football that should be studied by a lot of programs, including Tennessee." He reflected on Notre Dame team members appearing to show more respect in their approach to their opponents, their off-field behavior, and their own team. "To borrow a line from Weis—'We've really sold our team on the idea that the only thing that's important is the team.' "

So Many People to Welcome

Respect as a tangible strength is at the root of the mandate for hospitality that Alumni Association

director Chuck Lennon has shouted at pep rallies for years. Enjoy Notre Dame's hospitality, he tells the fans of the opposing team, "but don't mistake our hospitality as weakness."

The hospitality is necessarily served up in heaping helpings to friends and "opponents" alike. Far more than 100,000 people are on campus for any given gameday, although estimates vary from week to week based on the visiting teams involved and the perceived stakes of each individual contest.

At the most "micro" level, regardless of the number of spectators attracted by the contest, Notre Dame endeavors to show hospitality to the opposing team players themselves, along with their whole entourage. Observers say that many teams see their day in Notre Dame Stadium as a highlight of their own season, something to be savored as an experience and treasured as a memory, whether or not they win.

Visiting teams are offered an opportunity for a "walk-through" of the stadium—an orientation to the field of battle—when they arrive in South Bend. Groups like the band and cheerleaders have traditions for welcoming their counterparts from other schools. At the end of games against military academies, the Notre Dame team joins the opponents' fans in singing their school songs.

Of course, when the competition between Notre Dame and a team like the University of Southern California takes on extra dimensions of longevity and intensity, the hospitality is more clearly mixed with expressions of rivalry. The storied series that started against USC in 1926 has been memorialized by a shillelagh—a weapon of war from Ireland's past—that is claimed and adorned by each year's winning team. For each respective win, USC adds a ruby Trojan head, and Notre Dame adds an emerald leprechaun. The first shillelagh filled up with these jewels and was retired; it is now on display in the Joyce Center.

So Many People to Feed

Notre Dame's Food Services kicks into overdrive on a football weekend. This unit of the university provides food of one kind or another for up to

Jim "Skip" Sullivan '60 views the ND-USC shillelagh exhibited at the Sports Heritage Hall in the Joyce Center.

three hundred events or venues before, during, and after a typical game, says David Prentkowski, Food Services director. These events might include receptions or full dinners for the university's trustees and advisory councils, or for media personnel and their guests, or for a group of the visiting team's alumni.

Mustering that much food requires not only four hundred full-time employees, but also student workers and other part-timers, Prentkowski says. The weekend workforce totals perhaps twelve hundred, but double that figure if you're also counting all the concession stands—not only in the stadium, but at the Joyce Center, at on-campus arenas where other sports teams might be playing, and elsewhere. To deliver all the food and the complex catering services ordered, Prentkowski secures extra trucks to supplement his own fleet. "A lot of our on-call drivers are off-duty firefighters" who are comfortable handling large rigs, he says.

Under an unusual and popular program, concession stands are often assigned to groups from local churches, schools, charities, and other organizations. "They provide the labor and execute our plan," says Prentkowski, noting that Food Services provides these groups' supplies and training.

There are many other ways, too, in which Notre Dame shows its hospitality prowess on a gameday weekend. The Morris Inn provides many guest rooms and meals, as well as a backyard tent that features big-screen TVs and supplies of food and drink available for purchase in a kind of tailgate-for-the-masses. The Legends of Notre Dame restaurant and alehouse pub serves up food and TV screens—and restrooms—for paying customers. The DeBartolo Performing Arts Center often has world-class performers scheduled on gameday weekends, as well as throughout the year. The local golf courses have plenty of players who may favor tee times over kickoff times.

Kickoff Luncheon

The hospitality really hits its stride around noon on Friday, with a reasonably priced "Kickoff Luncheon" in the Joyce Center fieldhouse, attended by the head football coach, team members, dignitaries of various sorts, and hundreds of fans who have arrived early for the weekend. It's a great way to get in the mood for the game. Attendees find themselves in the audience for a casual but informative "talk show" hosted affably by local TV sportscaster Bob Nagle. One of the regular guests is coach Charlie Weis, and a few of the players usually get to practice their "interviewee" skills, all sharing their insights about the approaching game and related matters.

The luncheon traces its roots back to the Quarterback Club, which was co-founded by legendary Notre Dame coach Ara Parseghian and Charlie Sweeney in 1971. Charlie, a 1964 Notre Dame Law School graduate who also founded the Sweeney Law Firm and the *Blue and Gold Illustrated* fan newspaper, is the son of Chuck Sweeney, All-American end on Notre Dame's 1937 team. The idea of the club was partly to get together on Mondays and review the game of the preceding weekend. Those early luncheons featured Parseghian voicing over the 16-mm films.

Richard Conklin, who retired as associate vice president of University Relations early in this decade after many years of service to Notre Dame, recalled in an essay the story from past years of one fan who helped the diners get in the gameday spirit:

Holy Cross Sister Patricia Jean Garver left her mark on the Friday football luncheon at age 75. Receiving an impromptu call to the lectern before 1,500 people, the elderly nun mimicked Rockne in addressing the players. "You're going to go out there," she exhorted, "and you're going to line up, and you're going to look eyeball to eyeball with the guy across from you, and I'm telling you, you're going to tell them, 'Boy am I going to squash you!' " These were not exactly the words expected from a septuagenarian woman religious. Momentarily stunned, her audience then rose as one to give her a standing ovation. She later assured the players that sisters all over the country clutched Notre Dame football schedules, "and every Saturday morning you get more Hail Marys than Hershey's has candy bars." Sister Patricia Jean Garver also ended up with a game ball and a place in Notre Dame lore.

Oblates of Blues

Communities can be found everywhere on campus on gameday, but one "band of brothers" that many visitors will see, and hear, is actually a band, and at least the group's name suggests a virtuous, or virtuoso, kind of brotherhood. The Oblates of Blues are among the entertainers who perform outside the Eck Visitors Center on Saturday mornings. The Oblates comprise faculty members, graduate students, and graduates of the department of theology who just happen to love blues music.

An oblation is a donation or offering, usually to honor God. "Oblate" is the title for a lay or associate member of a Benedictine monastic community. The band has its origins at the School of Theology of St. John's Abbey and University, a Benedictine school in Collegeville, Minnesota.

"Screamin' Maxi" is one of the band's stars. He is Rev. Maxwell E. Johnson, an ordained

Lutheran minister who is also a professor of liturgical studies at Notre Dame. He plays guitar and performs vocals. Visitors will also hear vocals, harmonica, and percussion offered up by Rev. Hugh Page, an ordained Episcopal priest and Notre Dame's Walter Associate Professor of Theology. Page became dean of the First Year of Studies program in 2005.

That's the Ticket

If you're looking for signs and wonders on gameday, you'll certainly see the scalpers' "Need Tickets" signs all over town, and no wonder. The popularity of tickets for Notre Dame games has prompted its share of ticket-related marketing—and occasional mischief—outside appropriate box-office channels. The University announced in July 2006 that four 2006 home games ranked among the all-time top ten games for requests in the alumni ticket lottery. Notre Dame also warned fans of ticket scams that had multiplied for the 2006 season.

The school's ticket resale policy is strictly enforced by various means, including monitoring of ticket resale websites. The Notre Dame Counterfeit Ticket Task Force is on duty. US postal inspectors are present in the ticket office on gameday just in case fans have received duplicates to replace lost tickets and the appearance of a second set of tickets suggests that theft from the US mail might have taken place. According to Cappy Gagnon of the NDSP, there are roughly fifty to a hundred lost tickets at every home game, on average.

No Ticket Necessary Here

As if to prove that some of the best things in life are still free, many people who do not have tickets to the game still find that spending a Saturday afternoon at Notre Dame is a lot like a walk in the park. One typical (not intended as stereotypical) scenario is for a father and son to take in the game, while mothers and smaller kids take in the

beauty and mild temperatures (one hopes) of an autumn day.

Of course, no ticket is necessary for most of the day's activities, and many people make it their business all day simply to provide hospitality to those who want to see the campus and learn something about Notre Dame. The Eck Visitors Center offers showings of its eleven-minute video about the university. The center also offers campus tours to anyone who is interested. A number of undergraduates are engaged as tour guides, making numerous trips around campus.

If you're still interested in seeing the game, you can do that without a ticket, too. Locations in the LaFortune student center and the Joyce Center fieldhouse are just two of the places where you can watch the television coverage with hundreds of intense fans who feel that the walk in the park can wait.

President's Brunch

The invitation-only brunch held for University officials, benefactors, and distinguished guests is

Associate Vice President Rev. James McDonald, CSC *(left)*, speaks with Laetare Award winner and then-chair of the trustees Patrick McCartan and his wife, Lois.

one way to spend part of a gameday morning, if you're not inclined to be part of the throngs eating steak sandwiches or doing a hundred other things across campus. Besides the food served up at the breakfast, attendees also get a brief concert from a contingent of the Notre Dame Band.

Most Important Meal of the Day

There's another breakfast that Notre Dame serves up for its VIPs—Very Important Police, that is. Before their duties begin, the many members of numerous local departments who will play various security roles throughout gameday are shown hospitality in the form of a free, hot meal. Officers share information, discuss any last-minute changes, and review matters for the day.

A Busy Bookstore

One of the most bustling places on campus is the Hammes Notre Dame Bookstore in the Eck

Visitors Center. The bookstore serves as the gateway to gameday for many visitors.

Most of the thousands who come to shop at the store on any given football weekend are there to buy books, apparel, souvenirs, or all three, but the experience can easily go beyond shopping. People come to meet up with old friends, to have a snack, to discover a hard-to-find work of scholarship or religious item, to see sports figures and other celebrities who are signing books, and to be part of an event that makes new memories.

The number of book signings spanning Friday through Sunday can be significant. The upcoming weekend's visiting authors are listed in the free *Gridiron Graffiti* guide, and the store has a mailing list of people who have requested advance notice.

Even without any planning, a step into the bookstore lobby may bring an unexpected immersion into a broader past and present, including Notre Dame coaches, possibly President Emeritus Rev. Edward A. "Monk" Malloy, CSC, or celebrities from beyond the campus. The book signers enjoy the experience themselves, seeing people they haven't talked with in years and friends they didn't know they had. The immersion gets kicked up a notch if the cheerleaders, the leprechaun, or other student groups pay a visit.

Besides being open for a large part of the day, bookstore managers say they aim to make every guest's visit a pleasant one by having efficient procedures in place and plenty of full-time and part-time sales personnel who can point people to the latest academic publication or a particular kind of sweatshirt.

The current bookstore, opened in 1999 as part of the Eck Visitors Center near the main entrance to campus, is intended to serve as a resource for and a portal to the Notre Dame community, says James O'Connor, former director of the store who is now a regional manager with the Follett Higher Education Group, which manages the bookstore. The store is positioned as a destination point not only for campus regulars but for the greater South Bend community and beyond.

It's definitely a different place from the campus's previous bookstore, which stood at the current location of the Coleman-Morse Center. Run for many years by Brother Conan Moran, CSC, who was also known as "Brother Bookstore," the previous facility had limited weekend hours and much less space. But the legacy of caring deeply about books and about Notre Dame's distinctive community persists.

"The current bookstore is truly the beneficiary of those that came before us, like Brother Conan Moran," says O'Connor. "Our success has been

the result of academic excellence, religious experience, and the athletic tradition of the University of Notre Dame." The facility's own traditions have helped to build it into one of the premier collegiate bookstores, he says, with more than a million visitors every year surveying its broad and deep book offerings alongside its selection of Notre Dame gifts, clothing, and general merchandise.

As part of the University community with significant outreach off-campus, the bookstore has helped to raise money for such causes as Hannah & Friends, the Center for the Homeless, and a scholarship fund sponsored by spouses of Notre Dame and Saint Mary's College faculty.

The store has also given its name to one of the campus's spring semester traditions, Bookstore Basketball, partly because this annual competition used to be played on the basketball courts behind the old bookstore. Today, there are new and improved courts adjacent to the Eck Center facility, and the Hammes Notre Dame Bookstore Basketball Tournament is sponsored jointly by the bookstore and adidas. It has been dubbed "the largest outdoor 5-on-5 tournament in the world," according to the event's official website: "Over 500 teams comprised of students, faculty, and staff from Notre Dame, Saint Mary's College, and Holy Cross College participate in one of the most exciting sporting events on Notre Dame's campus."

Tackling Public Issues, Too

Visitors to campus on gameday are quickly reminded that their visit to a great American university can be an adventure for the intellect, too. A tradition of relatively recent vintage is the "Saturday Scholars" series of lectures—examinations of various topics, open free of charge to the public and usually featuring Notre Dame faculty. They are scheduled several hours before kickoff.

Emil Hofman *(standing)* engages in conversation with the audience at a gameday lecture held in his honor.

One such event, "The Role of Religion in Peacebuilding," held on November 4, 2006,

> Notre Dame estimates that Hofman taught more than 32,000 of its students, including thousands who are now physicians, engineers, and scientists.

before the North Carolina game, featured speakers from the Kroc Institute for International Studies: Kroc director R. Scott Appleby; John Paul Lederach, professor of international peacebuilding; and A. Rashied Omar, assistant professor of Islamic studies and peacebuilding. Even on gameday, the academic character of the university is on display for its visitors.

Another series of talks, the Dr. Tom Dooley Society lectures, also exercises minds on Saturday mornings. The Dooley Society is dedicated to supporting alumni of Notre Dame who work in the field of medicine, and its work also includes mentoring of students interested in the field. There is also an annual Emil T. Hofman Lecture—facilitated by Mark Walsh '69, a local physician—which honors the school's dean emeritus of the First Year of Studies and legendary professor of chemistry. The 2007 Hofman lecture featured a noted expert on rheumatology, and the audience gave an especially warm welcome to Hofman himself.

The Mess and the Cleanup

The policy issues discussed in scholarly talks may be messy, but they can't compare to the mess that is inevitably generated by a campus full of revelers. "It's just amazing how much trash is generated," says William Kirk, associate vice president for residence life. Shortly after the start of the game, a tractor circles the stadium assembling a train of garbage bins into which discarded beer cans and every other kind of rubbish has been quickly collected.

The challenge of trash continues during and after the game, in the stadium and beyond. The 2006 game against Michigan was said to generate a possible record (up to that point) of seventy-three giant bins of trash to be hauled away.

In the stands themselves, the job requires professional custodial service teams methodically working their way around the semi-lit stadium on Saturday night. Sunday brings a hangover of trash still to be picked up around campus, but much of the damage has already been undone by early in the day. By the time the weekend is over, the campus has returned to its largely pristine beauty.

During the 2007 football season, student volunteers started a new program called Gameday

> Notre Dame has been lucky to do without one factor that could add to the cleanup challenge, namely the seldom-seen arrival of a heavy snowfall on gameday.

Recycling, providing recycling opportunities for fans. On the day of the Michigan State game, the program collected some 1,200 pounds of material. This and other recycling efforts on campus use the slogan "It's easy bein' green at ND."

Meet the Press

John Heisler *(right)* oversees press box activities.

Every Notre Dame home game attracts a media corps of at least several hundred people, al-

though exact numbers will differ based on the records of the two teams. Keeping the print reporters, broadcasters, video and audio technicians, and backup staffs informed, equipped, and fed is an immense task.

What kinds of resources are the journalistic hoards looking for? John Heisler, senior associate athletics director and chief overseer of the stadium's third floor, or Media Level, gives this partial list: wireless Internet connections, game programs, rosters, game notes, transcriptions of coaches' interviews, and real-time video coverage of the games and press conferences.

What about food? The reporters have a great deal to choose from, including Port-a-Pit chicken, hot dogs, soup, "veggie" meal options, apples, popcorn, donuts, coffee, cider, soft drinks, and bottled water.

What else might contribute to the comfort of the corps? Besides all the other features already in place, air conditioning made its debut in the Media Level press box for the 2007 season.

Journalists know they're going to be treated with a high degree of professionalism at Notre Dame games partly be-

Sister Anthony Wargel, an Ursuline sister who has been the recipient of tickets to games as a gift from Notre Dame fans in Columbia, SC, was one of the limited number of guests invited to the Media Level during a game in 2006. She commented on the kindness shown to her by people she encountered throughout the Notre Dame community. "I've never had this kind of experience." She also acknowledged that she can't separate her religious values from her support for Notre Dame; she recalled the 2005 game against USC—the contest that has been called the game with two endings, and that ended with a tough loss for Notre Dame. "I was literally on my knees for the last six seconds of that game." She is shown here chatting with Doug Eads, a reporter from Somerset, KY.

cause of Heisler's own track record as longtime sports information director. This South Bend native is in the third decade of his service to Notre Dame athletics. He joined the staff in 1978 as assistant sports information director.

Heisler has authored or collaborated in the production of several books, and he has helped to edit a variety of publications, including twenty-five judged best in the nation by College Sports Information Directors of Amereica (CoSIDA) panels. In 2003, he was named to the CoSIDA Hall of Fame and received the Heisman Memorial Trophy Excellence Award in recognition of outstanding contributions to collegiate football. He also received the Special Presidential Award from Notre Dame President Rev. Edward Malloy, CSC, in 1994, and the Monogram Club awarded him an honorary monogram in 1991.

5 STADIUM AND STANDS

Celebrating Life on Many Levels

Notre Dame Stadium, built in 1930 and expanded in the 1990s, is one of those places that does not have to work hard to be great. There are bigger stadiums around the world that make a grander first impression, but this stadium lets a hundred other impressions—of its surroundings, of its history, of the event and all its participants—resonate within its walls and within the hearts of fans.

It has no jumbo television scoreboard. It has no commercial signage or giant logos on the field or in the end zones. It even lacks a fancy name, like "Knute Rockne Memorial Stadium," even though it is affectionately (and more or less accurately) called the House that Rockne Built. It is strangely silent as gameday begins, with tens

of thousands of people gradually entering orbit around it, and then it humbly and effectively fulfills its purpose, vibrating youthfully to the beat of the game and all the surrounding hoopla. Then, it falls silent again, standing by for its future while holding onto its past with dignity.

A Vast Panoply of Workers

Notre Dame Stadium is an architect's dream because it is organic, taking on the life and the love of the people who fill it. One is reminded of Paul's words: "Love is patient; love is kind. Love is not jealous. It does not put on airs. It is not snobbish. Love is never rude. It is not self-seeking, it is not prone to anger; neither does it brood over injuries. Love does not rejoice in what is wrong but rejoices in the truth. There is no limit to love's forbearance, to its trust, its hope, its power to endure" (1 Corinthians 13:4–7). There are hundreds of individuals who contribute their loving care to the stadium's heartbeat, making it beautiful and functional, keeping it safe and comfortable.

Take Dan Brazo, manager of athletic grounds, who makes sure that the playing field is well cared for and ready for every game. He's a naturalist who also serves as a curator helping to protect wildlife at Notre Dame's nearby Warren Golf Course. He and his groundskeeps preserve both the beauty and the efficacy of the stadium's playing field through year-round maintenance.

The stadium also offers silent tribute to the managers, the maintenance people, and all the people who are on duty before or after games. During the games, there are repair personnel standing by if a stadium elevator should stall; after all, the many people filling the various levels of the structure rely on their services. There are plumbers ready to address lavatory backups; even more people rely on *their* services. The list of stadium workers goes on and on—engineers, technicians, ushers, experts of all sorts. These people make it possible to connect a football stadium somehow with the love of a community of workers—and their love *of* community.

If love is quantifiable, there's a whole lot of it in the stadium on gameday. Cappy Gagnon, coordinator of stadium personnel, estimates that, while the stadium is known to have seating capacity for approximately eighty-one thousand people, there might be closer to eighty-six thousand people in the stadium at any one time. They include more than eight hundred ushers,

about four hundred band members, more than one hundred football players, and nine hundred people staffing the concession stands and other posts, from the police to the program-sellers to the first aid clinic staff.

A Focal Point for Honor

The stadium preserves many memories within and on its walls. Those Heisman winners are immortalized near Gate B. Panels on the walls near Gate A honor Irish players who have been consensus All-Americans. At Gate D, Notre Dame dedicated a new statue in 2007, honoring Ara Parseghian and showing him on the shoulders of players after their 1971 Cotton Bowl win.

Notre Dame's seven Heisman Trophy winners were honored in a special way during the 2006 season. Because the season inaugurated a seventh

annual home game, each game offered the opportunity to salute one of the winners out on the field during the pregame coin flip. The winners were also honored with their pictures on the tickets and program covers for each game. The Heisman list goes like this: Angelo Bertelli in 1943, Johnny Lujack in 1947, Leon Hart in 1949, John

John Huarte, 1964 Heisman winner, before a coin flip during the 2006 season.

Lattner in 1953, Paul Hornung in 1956, John Huarte in 1964, and Tim Brown in 1987.

God, Country, Notre Dame

Every year, the Alumni Association presents its Rev. William Corby, CSC, Award to an alumnus or alumna, living or deceased, for distinguished service in the military. The presentation is typically celebrated on the field during a home game against a military school opponent. In 2006, the Corby Award went to Retired US Navy Captain Jack J. Samar Jr. '71. Samar received his commission through Notre Dame's ROTC program.

It's also part of Notre Dame's hospitality to insert into its game with a military academy football team a program to honor military service. A flyover by military jets in formation, punctuating the band's performance of the national anthem, is another patriotic tradition.

Wee Hours Before the Big Game

Gameday starts very early, although most people aren't around yet to see it. The stadium is unlocked by the Notre Dame Security Police at five am so people with the appropriate clearances can start their various set-up activities. These include people who operate mobile concession stands, which are parked inside the stadium but then must be moved to their positions in the vicinity.

Cars that have been illegally parked overnight in the nearby lots are towed away so that tailgate regulars can start trickling in around six am.

A group of loyal alumni starts setting up the alumni tables in the Joyce Center around seven

Cappy Gagnon (*right*), coordinator of stadium personnel, and NDSP officer Tim Pitts.

am. Some of these loyal helpers have been doing this task for years, even making a predawn trek from Chicago to do so.

Wild

The electricity in the stands during a game is palpable, and it takes a variety of visible forms, especially in the student section. Students are perpetually standing and dutifully raising a din designed to short-circuit any offensive momentum that an opposing team might try to develop. At several points during the game, the students erupt into certain traditional cheers and gestures. They include the "W" (which easily made the transition from the coaching tenure of Tyrone Willingham to that of Charlie Weis, having previously morphed from the "L" of the Lou Holtz era), which accompanies the band's playing of the *1812 Overture*. The students also chop the air with their arms in time with the menacing beat of

the Darth Vader theme from *Star Wars*. And they wave their keys to signal a "key play."

Other Teams on the Field

A plain-clothes officer of the Notre Dame Security Police, who happens to be trained in dignitary protection, escorts coach Charlie Weis on and off the field and elsewhere on football weekends. He and others in the NDSP coordinate with various security officials, including sometimes even the Secret Service, to provide protection to high-ranking visitors inside and outside the stadium.

Many other scenes on the field remind one of the prodigious human energy that must go

into all the details of the game. For instance, there is the chain gang—those who assist the game officials by marking where a team begins its series and how far it must go to make a first down. At Notre Dame, that chain gang is made up of referees from local high schools. Some of the field assistants have been doing their jobs for thirty-five years or more, says Mike Danch, assistant athletics director.

The Green Jerseys

One of the "occasional traditions" that fans see on the field is what might be called the wearing of the green. The Fighting Irish customarily wear blue jerseys at home, but the option for switching to green jerseys for certain games has existed at least since the Rockne era and continues to the present day.

A perceived "jinx" was removed from the green outfits when they were worn in the 2006 Notre

Dame vs. Army game, from which Notre Dame emerged victorious. Coach Charlie Weis was quoted as saying that the shift to green was a kind of gift from the team and its coaching staff to the graduating senior players.

Prior to that victory, the Irish had donned the green for their sensational game against USC in 2005, but the game had gone sour for them in the closing seconds. The green had also suffered losses in a few games dating back into the 1990s. In earlier times, the green jerseys had developed a bit of a proud history of their own. According to an item on the CSTV.com website, green was prominent during the Frank Leahy coaching tenure, and in 1947 Heisman Trophy winner Johnny Lujack appeared on the cover of *Life* magazine wearing that color.

The team joined with adidas in honoring the thirtieth anniversary of Notre Dame's 1977 national championship team by wearing authentic green jerseys and gold pants—recalling the uniforms worn by the 1977 team—during the 2007 Notre Dame game against USC.

Police Presence

The police presence at gameday is a model of co-operation and coordination among officers from several different forces. The Notre Dame Security Police are joined by members of the South Bend Police Department, the Mishawaka Police Department, and the St. Joseph County Sheriff's Office, as well as Indiana state troopers. Some contract security is also hired for gameday. At any one time, more than one hundred police might be observed in the stadium itself, but that doesn't count the officers and civilian volunteers doing various jobs on- and off-campus, such as traffic management. And don't forget the Indiana Excise Police keeping an eye on tailgating activities and counterfeit tickets.

Most of the police on duty for the day gather for a morning briefing before beginning their

duties. Many other public safety personnel are on duty, including the Notre Dame Fire Department.

Security Monitors

The long arm of the law is assisted by cameras in various locations, including ones located on the stadium's lighting pylons that can stare down on activities in the parking lots and elsewhere. One person keeping watch on a variety of security video feeds is in a small stadium office. Among the places he can view is the stadium's public safety office, which unfortunately sees plenty of action during a typical game as violators of various laws are brought in for processing. If an unruly fan needs more than processing, there's a lock-up—a temporary waiting area where those arrested are held before transport to the St. Joseph County jail.

The Field of Medicine

Medical problems faced in the stadium's trio of first aid stations can include heat exhaustion, bee stings, ankle sprains, asthma, splinters, and occasionally a more severe health incident. During a game, stricken fans will find a number of beds for recuperation, with doctors and nurses on duty using a variety of resources for diagnosis and instant care.

"We are part of a group of two physicians, two nurses, two emergency medical team personnel, one radio operator, one support staffer, and four Red Cross volunteers who staff each first aid room," Dr. Stephen Anderson '68 says. There are three operational first aid rooms, one on the upper deck and two on the lower deck. Outside game time, nurse Kay Koziatek works at Elkhart General Hospital, and nurse Janet Kowalewski works at Our Lady of Peace Hospital, which is a

Dr. Stephen Anderson '68, an internist, is one of the healers on duty during the home games. In the photo, he is flanked from left to right by registered critical care nurses Kay Koziatek and Janet Kowalewski.

unit of St. Joseph Regional Medical Center, Anderson reported. Dr. Anderson shares duties with Dr. Mark Walsh '69, an emergency room physician at South Bend's Memorial Hospital.

"We pride ourselves on offering as comprehensive a first aid coverage as you are likely to find at any college football stadium," Anderson comments. "There are over sixty people who are part of the first aid team in the stadium."

The Wired World of Sports

In this age of instantaneous, multimedia communication, with scores of people—from coaches to cameramen, from police to TV producers, from firefighters to food providers, from scorekeepers to timekeepers—requiring completely reliable networked interaction for important messages that must be transmitted around the stadium or across the country, a team of technicians must remain on guard to ensure that all systems are "go," says Steve Ellis, director of integrated communications services (ICS).

His team supports the wireless headsets used by the coaching staff. Datacom services, such as video streaming systems and wireless networks, are maintained by technicians. The ICS works closely with NBC to ensure frequency coordina-

tion and other tasks. Cable TV experts ensure that the media and others have access to all necessary video.

Jerry Wray *(left)* and Mike Fitzpatrick stand beside some of the electronic infrastructure of the stadium.

The communication challenge is everywhere. "Few people know that the university's switchboard fields many calls on gameday, covering everything from 'What's the weather like?' to 'How do I get there?'" comments Ellis. A representative of AT&T is on hand to make sure that basic phone services are maintained.

Some people are keying in the information that gets posted on the stadium's scoreboard, while others are stationed in the press room entering play-by-play information on their laptops. Computer experts from Notre Dame's Office of Information Technology (OIT) are on duty to set up those systems and then to relay those statistics to the athletics department's website, und.com. That website translates the raw data into graphics and ensures good game coverage for those following the event via the Internet. The OIT is using not only a server to facilitate the transfers of information but also a laptop that constantly monitors und.com. Master programs for organizing all of this information must be updated for football and other sports.

University Level

The University Level of the press box is a gathering place for guests of the administration. It may not be the best place to become immersed in the excitement of the stadium, despite its panoramic view, but it does allow for immersion in university hospitality and friendly contact with a variety of VIPs. University President Rev. John Jenkins, CSC, has a private box, as does the chair of the Board of Trustees, and a third box is shared by Presidents Emeriti Hesburgh and Malloy.

The House of Ushers

When you arrive at the turnstiles to enter Notre Dame Stadium, you'll be welcomed to Notre Dame by one (or more) of the over eight hundred ushers who constitute perhaps the university's most distinctive and loyal cadre of gameday representatives. Many of them are locals, but others travel from nearly two dozen states to be part of a football weekend. It is said that no college has more ushers than Notre Dame on a gameday.

Some receive a stipend for their service, especially if their duties are more sensitive or managerial or if they preclude the individual from seeing the game, but a majority serve in a volunteer capacity. They hail from a few different generations, although their population skews to the older side. Approximately fifty end their service every year, with some earning retirement credentials after twenty-five years of ushering. "It's amazing how many of these guys have worked forty or fifty years," says Mike Danch, the assistant athletics director who manages stadium activities. There are several families who have three generations working as ushers during the same game, he adds.

Supervisors wear gold caps. Assistant supervisors wear blue caps. Captains wear white caps. The rank and file ushers wear gold baseball caps. They are standing by at every entrance to the stadium and every entrance to the stands, providing stewardship for the stadium and its attendees. They are also on duty at other venues—in the press box, in the Joyce Center, at corporate tailgates. A much smaller squad of ushers serves at other varsity sports venues.

One of their proudest gameday traditions is of relatively recent vintage. Ever since the terror attacks of 9/11, a group of ushers gathers inside the stadium at Gate D just before they open it to the crowd and sing "God Bless America."

NEIGHBORS

The South Bend Community

Notre Dame, as a private, residential university, provides many of the basic services that students require. But it exists within a larger community, with which it shares important ties. Those ties are strengthened on gameday, when crowds descend upon the surrounding city and when fans share their enthusiasm for the team and the school.

The Statistics of Town-Gown Synergy

The synergy between Notre Dame and gamedays on the one hand and South Bend and its surrounding area on the other hand is many-faceted.

The Knute Rockne statue outside the College Football Hall of Fame in downtown South Bend.

It has emotional, social, cultural, and governmental implications, but probably the most measurable impacts are economic. Even on this score, up-to-date statistics are hard to come by.

Gameday-related figures were reported by Notre Dame in a 2002 report on the university's overall economic impact on the surrounding community. Based on the 2001 football season, consultants estimated that 195,000 out-of-county visitors attending the six home games spent about $38 million, pumping about $6.3 million into the local economy on an average gameday weekend.

There's no doubt that that number has grown, thanks to factors like the addition of a seventh home game in 2006 and the extra hotel rooms constructed in the area, says Greg Ayers, who served as executive director of the South Bend/Mishawaka Convention and Visitors Bureau until the spring of 2007.

By 2007, South Bend was also poised to be the scene of a real estate boom. "Despite a dramatic downturn in residential real estate sales nationally, development of town houses, condominiums, villas, and condo-hotels is booming in the South Bend area," wrote reporter Margaret Fosmoe in the *South Bend Tribune* on March 18. "Developers and buyers say the trend is driven by proximity to Notre Dame, especially for home football games. Buyers include fans, alumni, employees, retirees, and parents of current students." This form of investment in the community exceeded $200 million, based on figures provided by developers, the newspaper reported.

Gameday weekends also bring numerous other sources of cash flow to the area. Homeowners rent rooms and parking space to visitors, for example, while local institutions like St. Joseph High School and Saint Mary's College also offer parking at their sites for a fee.

It is difficult, with so many disparate ways that gameday weekends bring money and development planners into the community, to determine precise figures. A 2007 report, accounting for numerous factors, estimated Notre Dame's yearly economic impact on the local county to be more than $870 million.

A Tale of Two Concession Stands

As extensive as its operations are on a gameday weekend, Food Services could not easily provide staffing for all of the concession stands in and around the stadium. Their solution—teaming up with various community groups to serve to fans the food that has been designated and supplied—is a win for the fans, and a win for Food Services. It is also a win for the concession stand operators: churches, schools, and other organizations that make a commission for their work, which supports their organizations and their often noteworthy goals.

The members of Olivet African Methodist Episcopal (AME) Church, for example, don't just make pork sandwiches, bratwursts, and hot dogs at their concession stand; they make friends, and they help to make young people's college dreams come true.

Thanks to money they raised in 2005 at their stand in the stadium concourse, they were able to give a teenager fifteen hundred dollars to support her first year at a historically black college, says Alma Powell, who coordinates the approximately ten church members who reported weekly to the indoor concession stand into which the group moved during the 2006 season. The money was in the form of a scholarship that Alma says memorializes the late Peggy Eskridge, the first African-American teacher in the South Bend Community Schools and a member of Olivet AME.

The church, by the way, was the first African-American congregation in South Bend, and it is located on Notre Dame Avenue just south of South Bend Avenue, Powell reports. Originally, the stand was staffed primarily by a small group of friends, but now a wider network of church members volunteer to work at the stand and have helped to build "a new camaraderie" within the congregation, says Alma.

The binding force of food and drink is not limited to the connections within the church community, she adds. She volunteers to handle the cash register because she enjoys meeting the customers, many of whom love to talk about their first visit to Notre Dame Stadium. Powell's husband is a long-time usher who worked initially without pay but has risen to be a paid supervisor of ushers in the student section. Because the Olivet stand is near the spot where a group of ushers sings "God Bless America" before opening the gates, they take special care of the ushers and of the regular customers who zero in on the pork sandwiches, Powell says.

Students of Brandywine High School in Niles, Michigan, meanwhile, derived a world of knowledge in 2006 from staffing a stadium concession stand with their economics teacher, Ron Bishop

(who has since moved to a different teaching position). They experienced the day-to-day life of a small business, learning about costs and benefits—including the cost of being very busy for several hours on Saturday, says Bishop. One benefit: "It's exciting for the kids to be at Notre Dame."

But that wasn't the only benefit. The approximately one thousand dollars that the group earned in commissions on gameday added up. By the end of the 2006 season it totaled enough to significantly defray the costs of a late-November field trip for selected students to Ecuador and the Galapagos Islands, says Bishop. The connection to economics? Studying the impact of tourism on these places, and meeting with officials from local and international businesses.

Bishop came up with the idea of offering his students on-site glimpses of global economics several years ago. Previous trips included Haiti and Costa Rica. Those excursions occurred before Brandywine had a concession stand. The students in 2006 got a chance to take ownership of their unique opportunity to a much greater extent, helping to earn the money required and learning even more—about keeping the books balanced and serving up the proper portion of nachos—from their teacher. "We can't thank Notre Dame enough," says Bishop.

South Bend as Fan Headquarters

South Bend has tried to entice visitors to spend more of their time and money downtown, adding "weekend tent parties" in the center of the city, adjacent to the College Football Hall of Fame and the South Bend Chocolate Cafe. Greg Ayers said he hoped that this would become an-

other gameday weekend tradition for many visitors, especially as the number of hotel rooms, restaurants, and possibly new condo-hotels that were on the drawing boards in 2006 increased.

Since 2004, the Visitor's Bureau has been operating a website—http://notredamefootball weekends.org—that can point visitors toward hotel rooms that are still available. The office also cooperates in the community distribution of *Gridiron Graffiti*, the free weekly handout produced by the Alumni Association and the athletics department summing up all the times and places of major events.

Most of those events are on-campus, and community boosters have envisioned additional promotions to attract visitors to the area's many off-campus sites of interest, like the new Studebaker National Museum. That would suggest that

visitors really should arrive Thursday night—
whether or not their hotel reservation requires a
three-night minimum—so they can take in the
city's sights on Friday.

Many fans and members of the extended
Notre Dame family already have established their
own favored itineraries for visits to the South
Bend/Mishawaka area. Favorite dining establish-
ments run the gamut of cuisines and locations,
too numerous to mention here, but they include
two South Bend restaurants that as of 2006 had
won the AAA's Four Diamond Award, the LaSalle
Grill and the Carriage House Dining Room.

The entertainment and lodging possibilities
do indeed trickle over the chronological bound-

aries of the weekend and the geographical boundaries of the city of South Bend. The Varsity Clubs of America all-suites hotel in Mishawaka expanded in 2007, building its reputation not only as one of the region's lodging sites but as the home of a Saturday morning radio broadcast prepping the whole community for the day's big game. There are additional radio broadcasts from other sites, and just about all the local media get caught up in the excitement.

Traffic and Traffic Management

Usually, one toll booth is perfectly sufficient to serve those motorists using the South Bend-Notre Dame exit off the Indiana Toll Road. Why are there more like half-a-dozen toll booths constructed at the exit? You can see the answer on gameday mornings, when all of the booths are in use and the traffic can still be backed up.

Notre Dame is said to benefit greatly from its proximity to the Chicago metropolitan area,

since gamedays attract not only Chicagoland-based Domers, but also the area's alumni from all the schools that Notre Dame confronts.

In general, the large number of police on gameday traffic duty and their accumulated experience in how to adjust traffic patterns have helped to keep tie-ups to a minimum, but it's still a challenge at the end of a game when thousands of satiated fans all want to move from the parking lots to the toll road simultaneously. For 2007, a new road was constructed connecting the toll road entrance to the White Field.

Atlantic Aviation: The Big Little Airport

Many people don't even realize that South Bend Regional Airport is home to a separate sort of mini-airport at its back door. The facility, called Corporate Wings prior to its sale to Atlantic Aviation in 2007, is the center for parking and refueling of private planes, and it can get very busy on gameday weekends.

As reported by the *Wall Street Journal*, the weekend of the 2005 home game against the University of Southern California topped the charts for Corporate Wings. By kickoff time, some 270 private jets had landed, breaking the previous record of 172.

During the summer of 2006, the St. Joseph County Airport Authority invested more than $700,000 to expand the space allotted for parking of private jets, says John Schalliol, the Authority's executive director. The private jet facility is "the first impression of our community to a very large number of persons. They have done an outstanding job for a number of years." They are especially valuable during the football season, when they handle an average of 80–110 aircraft and their passengers on gameday. That role, he notes, makes South Bend Regional Airport "one of the busiest airports in the country, even if it is for a very short time."

Transpo and the South Shore Railway

For those visitors with a smaller budget and shorter distance to traverse than the patrons of Atlantic Aviation, the South Shore Railway and

South Bend's Transpo bus system have been reliable ways to get to gameday. The South Shore Railway connects South Bend, Chicago, and points in between, while Transpo offers Stadium Express shuttles between downtown South Bend and the Notre Dame Bookstore.

Our Kind of Town . . .

Residents of South Bend have been showing their support for Notre Dame on gameday weekends for generations. They fly Notre Dame flags on their porches, throw parties in their homes, and spend the whole day—often, the whole week before the game—consuming media coverage and making the event a centerpiece of their friendly conversations.

"I don't know if Notre Dame knows the depth of loyalty among long-time South Bend resi-

Local resident Leslie Klusczinski proudly displays a Notre Dame flag on her porch.

dents," says Notre Dame Stadium announcer, and former WSBT-TV and WNDU-TV anchorman Mike Collins. "Their loyalist base is literally right here in South Bend—there's no question about it. Just walk around. I see people wearing every era of Notre Dame sweatshirts and jackets you can find, some that go back 30 years. . . . I'm talking about people on the West Side, the South Side. People come up to me from every background, every ethnic group, to talk about Notre Dame football."

College Football Hall of Fame

The College Football Hall of Fame moved to South Bend in 1995, lured by the city from its previous home near Cincinnati. With its "Gridiron Plaza" outside and a unique underground museum inside, this distinctive downtown landmark often welcomes Notre Dame's opposing teams as visitors.

The Hall of Fame is one symbol of South Bend's embrace of college football in general, not

exclusively Notre Dame football. One should note that "Hail to the Victors," the rousing football fight song of the University of Michigan, was written in 1898 by Louis Elbel, a South Bend native. He is commemorated in a plaque near the Hall of Fame on Michigan Street.

The Hall of Fame faced some financial rough-going during its early years in South Bend, but then–executive director Rick Walls announced that it had been profitable in 2006 thanks to boosts in revenues, as reported in the *South Bend Tribune* on May 10, 2007. Event revenues were up 40 percent in 2006, and attendance was up 10 percent to 66,500 visitors. Notre Dame helps to promote the Hall of Fame on gamedays through materials published in the game programs and announcements made at weekend events.

Here Comes the Band

Local residents who aren't attending the game or who are already popping their popcorn at home as kickoff approaches still have a chance to enjoy the Notre Dame Band's fresh-weekly repertoire for free. They can come to a parking lot south of the Joyce Center on a late Friday afternoon and watch the Band perform in its grand outdoor "dress rehearsal."

Knights of Columbus Smokers

Probably the oldest tradition bringing the Notre Dame and South Bend communities together on every gameday weekend is the Knights of Columbus Smoker, held after the pep rallies on Friday evenings at the Sacred Heart Parish Center on campus. The Smoker, now a smoke-free and family-friendly event, was started in the mid-1940s when director of athletics Moose Krause asked the Knights of South Bend's Council 553 (the Santa Maria Council) to hold events that would promote attendance at the games. Elmer Danch, the father of today's assistant director of athletics and football gameday manager Mike Danch, was the council's Grand Knight around that time.

Legendary coach Ara Parseghian was one of the celebrities known to make appearances at the Smoker, and t-shirt sales at the events have allowed the Knights to make regular donations to the Ara Parseghian Medical Research Foundation.

The Knights served up a party that has been going strong ever since, providing a unique, casual setting for townspeople and visitors alike to enjoy bratwursts and beer while immersing themselves in football history, analyses, and predictions. These come in the form of short talks given by guest speakers who range from Notre Dame coaches to other Notre Dame celebrities of the past and present to media people to leaders from the visiting team. The warm and attentive welcomes given to the visiting team fans personify the tradition of hospitality that surrounds gameday.

Dan Modak, a member of Notre Dame's 1949 national championship team, leads a cheer with the crowd at a Knights of Columbus Smoker. Jack Landry, Ed Fay, and Jerry Begley look on.

These days, the events are emceed and coordinated by Council 553 member and Past Grand Knight Steve Filbert, who says he grew up in nearby Elkhart developing his love for Notre Dame through attendance at the local Catholic school. He credits his wife Mary with the persistence and persuasive power that continue to draw top-notch speakers for the Smokers. The Knights keep the admission price down to a bare minimum and don't offer honoraria to the speakers, but a free bratwurst meal is offered and three or four enthusiastic speakers are always lined up for every gathering.

Now that the Smokers are hardly the "only game in town" for visitors seeking entertainment on the Friday before the game, attendance is nowhere near the peaks reached in earlier decades when more than 1,000 people reportedly would fill the Knights' downtown council building with raucous good times and cigar smoke. But attendance is still a tradition that many Knights and other fans adhere to faithfully. Among the regulars has been Red Mack, who played for Notre Dame in the 1950s and later played for the Green Bay Packers.

The Filberts are constantly promoting attendance through invitations to Notre Dame alumni clubs around the country and other means. "Our whole goal is to keep increasing the quality and spreading the word around," says Filbert. He pumped up his own enthusiasm by participating in the Notre Dame Football Fantasy Camp in the summer of 2007.

Hannah & Friends

The "Hannah's Hands" towels that fans received free of charge and waved in the air at the 2006 Notre Dame-Penn State game were a symbol of many connections between Notre Dame football and enthusiastic displays of charity shown through organizations, communities, and individuals.

The towels called attention to Hannah & Friends, the foundation established by Charlie and Maura Weis to provide a better quality of life for children and adults with special needs. Another basic goal is to spread "awareness and compassion" for all those with special needs. The Helping Hands campaign provides grants for low- and moderate-income families caring for special-needs adults and children.

More than one hundred students from several Notre Dame residence halls volunteered to distribute seventy-five thousand "Hannah's Hands" towels at the Penn State game. Coach Weis has said the hands represent Hannah's support for the Notre Dame team and

Hannah & Friends is named for Hannah Weis, the daughter born to Charlie and Maura in 1995 and later diagnosed with global developmental delay. The Weises' son, Charlie Jr., is one of the foundation's supporters, and he has raised money with his own "Charlie Jr.'s Army Reserve" t-shirts.

symbolize the connection with all individuals who have special needs and who may not be able to attend sporting events in person. The website und.com, the exclusive Internet home for the athletics department, underwrote the cost of the towels.

The Foundation is providing funding to construct and operate a thirty-acre farm in the South Bend area where a residential community for adults with special needs can live in group homes. On April 17, 2007, the Weises attended the Human Rights Awareness Day luncheon at South Bend's Century Center. As reported by the *South Bend Tribune*, Maura received a service award from the South Bend Human Rights Commission, and the coach addressed the audience about what he had learned from his wife and from the experiences their family had shared in recent years. The act of helping others had been transformed from a consideration touching upon a busy coaching career to a top-of-mind reality that has "helped complete our lives," Coach Weis was quoted as saying.

Hannah & Friends is part of an annual fundraiser called the Notre Dame Coaches' Kickoff for Charity, a "team effort" that also raises money for the Holtz Charitable Foundation and the Ara Parseghian Medical Research Foundation. Notre Dame alumnus Regis Philbin served as the emcee at the first Kickoff event, held in New York in 2006. It raised over one million dollars for the three foundations, the Hannah & Friends newsletter reported.

Charity Unites Town and Gown

Hannah & Friends has rapidly become the best known charity connecting the football team to

South Bend. But charitable community connections have long been part of the ethos of Notre Dame athletics, says Harold Swanagan, a member of the class of '02 who captained the university's basketball team and who now oversees much of the local athletic goodwill as coordinator of student welfare and development.

This work is based on Notre Dame's commitment to provide the University's athletes with a balanced experience that includes academic excellence, athletic success, career preparation, community involvement, and personal development. "We build relationships with athletes on every team" so they can come in and talk about their interests and concerns, Swanagan says. The satisfaction of being well-rounded usually includes some form of service. "To be a top athlete, you've got to be a contender on the field, but you've also got to be able to contribute something to the community." He estimates that 90 percent of the athletes in the University's various varsity sports programs do some kind of commu-

Harold Swanagan at a football-gameday practice for the basketball team.

nity service, ranging from tutoring or mentoring young people to visiting schools and hospitals.

Through one program, called "Tackle the Arts," members of the football team gather at the Stepan Center on a summer day with about a hundred kids from the local Boys and Girls Clubs and other organizations, and they work on various artistic projects with them. These include music, painting, poetry, and photography. The athletes act as role models, showing another side of their own talents while encouraging the youngsters to exercise their own artistic abilities. Brady Quinn chaired the event in the summer of 2006.

Another program, Fighting Irish Fight for Life, connects all student teams—not just footballers—to patients in Memorial Hospital's pediatric oncology ward. In a sense, teams often "adopt" young cancer patients and offer spirit-lifting camaraderie, sometimes building long-term relationships.

It was through this program in 2005 that Charlie Weis learned about and visited ten-year-old Montana Mazurkiewicz, who was dying of a brain tumor. Invited to call the first offensive play for the upcoming game, Montana told Weis the Fighting Irish should pass to the right. The boy died a day and a half after the visit, but Weis and the team did not forget when gameday in Seattle against Washington arrived. They successfully passed to the right, as promised, even though poor field position dictated against such a play, and Weis later returned to the family and gave them the game ball, signed by the whole team.

Extending Charity

Weis and team have also continued Notre Dame's receptivity to the national Make-A-Wish

Foundation, which helps to make the arrangements for granting the wishes of young people with life-threatening conditions. Jennifer Laiber, a staff member in the university's Office of Public Affairs and Communication, happened to pick up a Make-A-Wish request when it arrived in the office fax machine in 2000. After facilitating the response to that first request, she saw the beauty of the program and has become a northern Indiana wish granter for the foundation.

"I've done eight wishes," said Laiber in early 2007, noting that a few of them involved Notre Dame, where members of teams—and the broader University family—have "gone one step extra" to try to make memorable responses possible. In one case in 2006, she was one of the hosts for an eight-year-old who had wished to attend a Notre Dame football game. The experience of spending a day with the boy and his family touched her deeply. When the boy died of leukemia shortly after Christmas, she drove out to attend his funeral in a town near Buffalo, NY.

Richard Conklin, former associate vice president for University Relations, recalled in an essay the story of another Make-a-Wish recipient who spoke at a pep rally in 2000:

> Scott Delgadillo was fighting leukemia when he successfully asked the Make-a-Wish Foundation if he could fulfill a lifelong dream of attending a Notre Dame football weekend. He had dinner with the team Friday and was asked jokingly if he were ready to speak at the pep rally. "Yeah," he unexpectedly replied. The normally raucous crowd was quiet when Scott introduced himself and told of his battle with cancer. He talked in a soft voice about hope and courage, faith and spirit. "As long as you have a positive attitude," he said, "you can go anywhere you want. Notre

Dame has inspired me." There were tears in the Joyce Center that September night as Scott promised to return to Notre Dame. The next day, he received the game ball from the gridiron victory.

The Notre Dame family adopted Scott, sending e-mails, letters, memorabilia, and prayers to him in a San Diego hospital. He responded in a letter to the campus newspaper which thanked Notre Dame people for their kindness and closed with the words, "Go Irish." Scott died four months after his inspiring words at the pep rally, but he did return to Notre Dame as promised. At the wish of his parents, his body was flown back to campus for a Mass in Sacred Heart Basilica.

GOLDEN FAME

Notre Dame's Nationwide Attention and Role

Notre Dame is known nationwide. For many people, the football team may seem to be the sole reason why Notre Dame receives so much national exposure. But Notre Dame actively promotes itself through other means as well. In fact, athletics has opened up windows of opportunity for charity and character formation to a broader group of people than merely its own athletes.

From Obscurity to National Fame

Notre Dame, a relatively small college in the Midwest, became nationally known in the 1910s and 1920s thanks to a confluence of factors, as

described in *Notre Dame: 100 Years*. One factor was certainly Knute Rockne, first as a player and later as coach. Also, because other regional universities with strong football programs kept Notre Dame out of their conference, the Fighting Irish were "forced to go to the East and the Far West for games" (*Notre Dame: 100 years*, 300). After compiling a record of competence, and with help from eager, supportive Catholic audiences for away games, Notre Dame developed the reputation of being a powerful, profitable drawing card against whom many schools were happy to compete.

That golden fame has taken Notre Dame a long way, and in more recent years the national media have picked up on the reputation and run with it. NBC's contract relationship with Notre Dame began in 1991, and the latest contract extends through 2010. The parties don't release financial terms of the contract. As reported at CSTV.com, the University has said that most of the proceeds go to an endowment supporting student financial aid. Indeed, as of 2006, nearly 1,700 Notre Dame undergraduates had been awarded more than $15 million in aid, and more than $10 million from NBC revenues had endowed doctoral fellowships in the Graduate School and MBA scholarships in the Mendoza College of Business.

In 2006, at a halftime ceremony during the Notre Dame-Purdue game, the Monogram Club presented NBC Universal Sports and Olympics chairman Dick Ebersol and NBC Universal Sports president Ken Schanzer with honorary monograms. Ebersol was also presented the flag that flew over Notre Dame Stadium on Nov. 5, 2005, when he and his family were part of the flag presentation prior to the Notre Dame-Tennessee game.

Big Names Visiting and Giving:
Hannah Storm and Chicago

Among the celebrities with a high gameday profile in 2006 were CBS News "Early Show" anchorwoman Hannah Storm '83 and the band Chicago.

Storm signed copies of her new book, *Notre Dame Inspirations: The University's Most Successful Alumni Talk About Life, Spirituality, Football—and Everything Else Under the Dome*. She previously won fame as a TV sports journalist and authored *Go Girl! Raising Healthy, Confident, and Successful Girls Through Sports*.

Proceeds from *Notre Dame Inspirations* partially fund a new Hannah Storm journalism internship through the Notre Dame Alumni Association. In

Hannah Storm signing copies of her book about Notre Dame.

The band Chicago performs on the field at half-time with the Band of the Fighting Irish.

2007, sophomore Jessica Bruno was selected as the first recipient of the internship, under which she assisted with the Alumni Association's communication and publication activities.

Chicago let its music tell its story, which dates back to its founding in its namesake city forty-plus years ago. They performed with the Notre Dame Marching Band during halftime of the 2006 game with the University of North Carolina. The band's manager is Peter Schivarelli, who played football for Notre Dame in the 1960s and 1970s. Chicago donates a percentage of its concert ticket sales to Hannah & Friends and the Ara Parseghian Medical Research Foundation.

New Media: CSTV

Notre Dame has kept pace with the rapid developments in communication as more and more

people are using the Internet to follow their favorite teams in greater depth, in real time, with video as well as text. As the 2006 season began, the principal website for Irish athletics fans, und.com, began providing an expanded menu of event coverage and features—all free of charge.

The und.com website, which began in 1995, is now an official partner with CBS-owned CSTV.com, which has been billed as "the most trafficked college sports website," with a network of hundreds of official athletic sites for universities and colleges. College Sports Television exists on cable and satellite TV, as well as on the Internet, covering a panoply of games from various college sports, but und.com maintains its own mission of streaming content.

In 2006, after the retirement of Jack Lorri, the longtime Notre Dame men's basketball radio play-by-play announcer, Notre Dame Sports Properties hired Jack Nolan as director of media productions, with his assignments including basketball play-by-play and various hosting duties for original programming for broadcast and the Web. Nolan had already been known as the color commentator for basketball and as an anchor-man on WNDU-TV.

Notre Dame Sports Properties, an entity separate from the university, also hired Alan Wasielewski as director of digital media. Wasielewski, a South Bend native and member of the Notre Dame class of 2000, previously served as assistant sports information director.

The aggressive move into Internet programming was a timely reflection of the Web's rapid growth as a source of video-on-demand. When Notre Dame played an away game at the Air Force Academy in 2006, coverage rights were held by CSTV, not NBC or ESPN, so local fans without the usual access to television coverage plunged into the new media universe. In August 2007, Comcast and Notre Dame announced the launch of an on-demand service covering Notre Dame sporting events on digital cable. It provides about 70 percent of the und.com content.

Brand Name, Brand Fame

If fame could be measured monetarily, Forbes.com would say that the fame of the Notre Dame football team is golden indeed. The website reported in 2007 that, by its metrics, the team was worth $101 million, more than any other football squad in the country. The estimate is based on several factors: the team's contributions to the university's athletics department and to academic uses, as well as sales revenues for South Bend and surrounding areas. Part of Notre Dame's advantage, *Forbes* says, is the $9 million annual broadcasting fee paid by NBC—"by far the most for any team." According to the website, based on figures from the 2006–07 fiscal year, the team pumped $21.1 million into the University

for academic use. The website reported in 2006
that $23.5 million went to the athletics depart-
ment for sports other than football and $57 mil-
lion in incremental sales to the surrounding
communities.

The University received another commerce-
minded compliment from *SportsBusiness Journal*,
which reported in late 2006 that its reader poll
had given top ranking to the Notre Dame "brand."
When readers were asked, "What university is the
top brand in college sports?" the school received
40.7 percent of the 1,251 votes. Michigan and
Duke came in second and third, respectively.

Another, somewhat less quantifiable indicator
of Notre Dame football's fame came when General Mills featured the university in the much-
coveted spot on its Wheaties cereal box. Wheaties
brands itself as "the Breakfast of Champions."

For some fans who can go far beyond breakfast time in expressing their brand loyalty, Notre
Dame Football Fantasy Camp has become in-
creasingly popular—so much so that a second
session was added during the summer of 2007.

Each four-day session offers spots for "players" and "honorary coaches" who undergo training and other experiences like those of the Fighting Irish football team, culminating in a "fantasy game" in Notre Dame Stadium. Members of the real team's coaching staff work with the participants, joined by former players. Coach Charlie Weis addressed both sessions. In 2007, a "Fantasy Bowl" was inaugurated to pit the Notre Dame Fantasy Camp against the Nittany Lions Fantasy Camp.

This tradition was initiated in 2003 by former Notre Dame quarterback Pat Steenberge '73, whose Global Football company is part of an organization providing amateur athletes around the world with opportunities to compete with each other and learn more about other cultures. Revenues from the Notre Dame Football Fantasy Camp go partly to benefit a need-based scholarship fund for sons and daughters of Monogram Club members attending Notre Dame.

In other programs that are geared less toward fantasy than toward personal formation for a future in athletics, the summer also brings opportunities for boys to get a taste of Notre Dame football and the environment of big-time college sports. The Notre Dame Summer Football Camp attracts young athletes who will be entering the seventh through twelfth grades. The Notre Dame Football Youth Day Camp gives boys in the third through sixth grades a few half-days of initial experience.

Charity on a Grand Scale: Katrina

Notre Dame's athletic program has become well-known for the good work that players do off the field as well as on the field. The university's policy of encouraging athletes to balance their sports lives with academic excellence and compassionate service was in clear, consistent view between 2005 and 2007 as many students—athletes and non-athletes alike—joined with other members of the Notre Dame family to respond in the aftermath of hurricane Katrina's devastating blow against New Orleans and the region around it.

Highlights in the long campaign of compassion included Father Jenkins' nationally televised appeal to support those affected by Katrina before a football game in 2005. More than three hundred students, alumni, staff, and administrators participated in service events in and around New Orleans on January 2, 2007, as the football team prepared to play in the Sugar Bowl. Particular activities were organized by Notre Dame's Alumni Association and the Center for Social Concerns.

In October 2006, fifteen student-athletes and five athletics department administrators, including director of athletics Kevin White, spent fall break working on repair projects in New Orleans. Also in October, Notre Dame was one of nine schools in the nation honored with a Katrina Compassion Award for Excellence in Hurricane Relief Service from the Corporation for National and Community Service.

The time for compassion is never past, and football games provide just some of the opportunities for expressing compassion that the Notre Dame community naturally and frequently seizes. At the time of the Blue-Gold Game on April 21, 2007, the tragedy on everybody's mind was the April 16 shooting of thirty-two people by a gunman on the campus of Virginia Tech. The hoopla of the game gave way to a moment of silence for the victims of the tragedy.

Play Like a Champion

A promotional video that was broadcast on national television during the games of the 2006 season celebrated the connection that so many Domers feel to the timeless summons to "Play Like a Champion Today." The video showed several alumni, highly respected figures in their respective career fields, following the football team's lead in touching signs that proclaimed "Research Like a Champion Today" or "Heal Like a Champion Today."

The original "Play Like a Champion Today" sign dates back to the 1980s, according to a story by Associated Press reporter Tom Coyne. Coach Lou Holtz reportedly wanted a blue and gold sign to be made with those words that would inspire his players. He had found records of such a sign existing in the past, but no one could remember when it had been posted or who was responsible for creating the sign or the slogan, Coyne reported. He quoted Holtz as saying, "I'm going to put it in the same place and everybody is

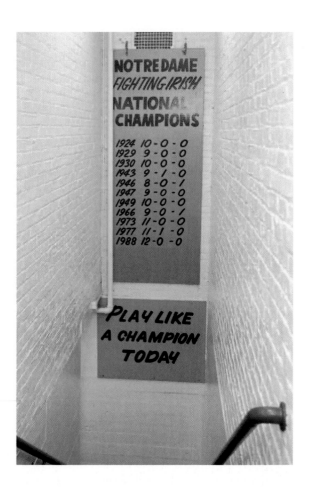

going to hit it on the way out to the field to remind them of all the sacrifices they have made, their families have made, and other people have made for them to be there."

The job fell to Notre Dame sign-maker Laurie Wenger, who produced the four-foot-high, three-foot-wide wooden sign in about a week, according to Coyne. The team's practice of hitting the sign became widely known in 1991 when NBC put a camera in the locker room tunnel, senior associate athletics director John Heisler told Coyne. Wenger said the first person to ask her for a copy of the sign was Rudy Ruettiger. Now, Coyne reported, Laurie and her husband Ron have secured a trademark and started a business selling screenprinted signs and other items bearing the slogan.

A replica of the sign goes on the road with the team.

Pray Like a Champion

One site on campus where students have embraced a similar message of accountability and aspiration is Old College, the oldest building on campus. It now serves as the residence for the community of undergraduates who are considering a vocation to the priesthood in the Congregation of Holy Cross. These students enjoy a daily inspiration suspended over the stairway—a sign urging them to "Pray Like a Champion Today."

Modifications to sign approved by PLACT, Inc.

"The men here at Old College take prayer very seriously," says Rev. Kevin Russeau, CSC, rector at this residence hall. "It anchors us." The building includes a chapel in which the community of young aspirants prays three times a day.

The theme of championship here has come to mean not only the drive to excel in and through their daily practices of prayer, but also to make prayer a key component of a well-balanced life. Notre Dame was founded with the intent of "forming good character"—educating both hearts and minds, Father Russeau says. "We work hard, we play hard, and we pray hard."

And gameday reflects and reinforces that combination on campus, he adds. "It's very clear that, win or lose, prayer is an essential part of the experience."

Sports as Ministry:
Coaching Coaches Everywhere

The "Play Like a Champion Today" message resonates with people everywhere, and it has found an especially welcoming audience among administrators, coaches, and parents involved in the athletics programs of Catholic grade schools. This group, like much of the general public, has been distressed by recent trends in youth sports like "parent rage" at games and the pressure to place winning above the good of the child and the lessons of good sportsmanship.

Clark Power, a professor in Notre Dame's Program of Liberal Studies, concurrent professor in the department of psychology, and co-founder of the Center for Ethical Education, has been reaching out to this audience through the "Play Like a Champion Today Educational Series" (PLC). The program, developed by experts in educational de-

Professor Clark Power shows a product of the "Play Like a Champion" initiative.

velopment and sports psychology, uses interactive workshops at the school and team level to address the priorities, attitudes, and skills that shape constructive youth sports activities.

He and his Center for Ethical Education colleagues, with the assistance of Notre Dame coaches and athletics department administrators, developed the Sports as Ministry Initiative to integrate "Play Like a Champion" principles with lessons about Christian spiritual growth and sacramental consciousness. After a pilot program at St. Joseph Grade School in South Bend during the 2005-06 academic year, the Sports as Ministry (SAM) Initiative fanned out to a number of dioceses and parishes around the country and in Canada. In June 2007, the Center held its second annual Play Like a Champion Today Sports as Ministry Leadership Conference, with representatives of several dioceses around the country attending to become certified trainers.

"Ministry is a form of service in the name of the Church," says the *PLC Program Overview*. "At the most basic level, the coach's ministry is to serve young people by helping them learn how to be more Christ-like through organized sports."

The Champion and Catholicism

Champion. "It's a good, rich word," says Power. It connotes being a good teammate, being considerate of others, taking responsibility. It suggests "I'm going to give the very best."

Gerry Faust, who coached Notre Dame from 1981 to 1985, has been quoted as a promoter of the "champion" message, and this inspiring author and speaker has continued to regularly attend Notre Dame games. "The word 'champion' means you're the best," says Faust. "You're a bar above the rest. When you play that way, you're going to be the best, and if you give your best, that's all you can ask of a person."

There's also something active and energizing, invigorating and celebratory, when one sees a

Former Notre Dame football coach Gerry Faust *(left)* enjoys a laugh with Chuck Lennon before a game.

champion at work, Power adds. Feats of athletic excellence excite others and prompt others to participate vicariously, perhaps even to feel a participation with others. "It's just great to see a member of our species do something wonderful."

What's more, we can watch champions go through the universal human experience of struggle and emerge successful. Athletic competition at a high level is "a great way of playing out life and experiencing, even after a devastating loss, hope." Perhaps an absence of hope is one reason why some students or some school communities don't seem to show the championship qualities but rather fall into the trends of violence and bad attitudes on the field or parent rage in the stands.

The linkage of the champion stance to hopefulness and a sense of human dignity is one reason why the Catholic Church and its various institutions are taking more interest in the pursuit of sports excellence, Power says. In November 2006, he was invited to participate in a seminar at the Vatican titled "The Christian Mission Within the Field of Sport Today." The seminar was organized by the church and sport office of the Pontifical Council for the Laity. Pope John Paul II (who, by the way, was awarded an honorary monogram by Notre Dame's Monogram Club) established that office in 2004.

Recognizing the Power of Sports

"Playing sports has become very important today, since it can encourage young people to develop important values such as loyalty, perseverance, friendship, sharing, and solidarity," the Vatican proclaimed in 2000, in a Jubilee Year address to the world's athletes (as reported in the book *The Catholic Ideal: Exercise and Sports*, Robert Feeney,

Aquinas Press, 2006). Sports are a defining phenomenon of the modern era, "capable of interpreting humanity's new needs and new expectations."

Power notes that the Vatican recognizes the role of modern media in increasing the potential for sports to do good. "It's something that the whole world can watch simultaneously."

Power's *PLC Program Overview* echoes one of the messages that the Church no doubt wants to communicate to the modern culture when it talks about coaching as ministry. "This means the coaches will help the players to see their play as a response to God's goodness and grace and to see their team as a part of the Church—as 'the Church playing.' From a theological standpoint, play can be one of the purest forms of worship. Play is a celebration of God's creation. Sport is a celebration of the physical dimension of creation."

Such theology seems to be on a firm footing, not only regarding the Church playing but also the Church Militant. The New Testament has its share of sports metaphors. Paul says in his epistle to Timothy: "I have fought the good fight, I have finished the race, I have kept the faith" (2 Timothy 4:7).

Interestingly, the verb "to champion" also can mean advocating for, or representing. And here is an area where Power has seen the ability of a champion-minded institution to add authority and validity to the message he is bringing to coaches. The university he has served for more than a quarter of a century is known for its ideals and sincerity and has withstood scrutiny of its willingness to walk the talk, he says: "Notre Dame *stands* for something."

PEOPLE ARE THE KEY

Personifying the Connections

We have seen throughout this book that a variety of communities make possible the gameday experience that so many people enjoy. Those communities come in the form of teams: the football team, the cheer squad, the concession workers, pastoral staff—and the list goes on. But within those teams, individuals must perform their duties as well. Just as in the microcosm of football, wherein each player must perform his duty—blocking, tackling, throwing the pass— for the team to succeed, so too must all the individuals play their part outside the stadium. The stories of those individuals enrich the story of gameday.

The Blue-Gold Game started out chiefly as an "old-timers game," but it now features the current team players split into two warring sides. The fact that those two sides get their own symbolic coaches—Lou Holtz (*right*) and Ara Parseghian in the 2007 game—maintains a powerful "old timers" touch of celebrating legacy.

Players as a Part of a Team

There are no names on the jerseys of Notre Dame football players. It's all about the team. But it's clear that the team relies on many individuals each achieving their personal best and bringing their own unique gifts to the total performance.

The close ties between individuals and between the team and its individual players often persist through their lifetimes. Former players can sometimes be found on the sidelines with the current team. They also return for the flag football games that are part of the Blue-Gold festivities every spring, and the especially fortunate alums return for national championship reunions.

The Team around the Game

The same melding of individual and group effort is true of gameday as a whole, with the group effort magnified on an incredible scale. Mike Danch, assistant athletics director for facilities, has been manager of all stadium activities on gamedays since 1997, and he knows what it's like to coordinate the efforts of roughly four thousand to five thousand people, some paid and some volunteer, who contribute in one way or another to the stadium phenomenon.

"It's not something you take for granted," he says, noting his appreciation for "all the management skills" that people are investing simply because "they really care about Notre Dame." These people know their jobs and do them well. "The challenge is to make sure that everybody is on the same page." One reason why everything must go according to script is the recognition that, for at least a percentage of every gameday's crowd, this is their first—maybe their only—experience of a Notre Dame football game, an experience that Danch wants to be memorable for its excellence. "That's a challenge for all of us on campus."

The number of details to be handled is prodigious. For example, weather conditions have to be monitored, starting a couple of days before gameday. While the "Victory March" may imagine shaking down the thunder, it's not meteorologically desirable. An actual thunderstorm over the stadium would require fans to take shelter, and 2006 marked the first time in Danch's experience that fans had to be warned of the possibility during a game as lightning bolts became visible on the horizon. "We lucked out," he says, and the lightning maintained a safe distance during the game.

Counting everyone and every task related to the stadium experience, the workday stretches from five am to at least ten pm. In some ways, the hours leading up to the game are the toughest, considering all the preparations and precautions, says Danch. "You're thrilled to get to the kickoff. Everything builds to that kickoff moment." The adrenaline of management doesn't stop flowing until after the game, though. "In victory, if things have gone well, there is a sense of relief."

Of course, the phenomenon of masses of people supporting an even bigger mass of people all for the sake of Notre Dame has to impress those visitors who are new to the school. It's no wonder that gamedays are important recruiting tools for prospective student-athletes, whom coaches in all of the various varsity sports want to lure. This is another way in which Notre Dame football is all about people: demonstrating the university's special love of sport and sportsmanship to those who will constitute the future of this showcase.

Family Connections:
Mike and Elmer Danch

When one asks the coordinator behind the scenes of this showcase about his own fondest memories, Mike Danch focuses on the human element of sport, even to the point of remembering an event that had nothing to do with football but everything to do with Notre Dame's outreach to others. He recalls when the stadium hosted the 1987 international Special Olympics, which featured a celebrity-studded TV broadcast of the opening ceremonies. On that grand day, four thousand Special Olympians marched onto the field in another one of those events that had to reflect excellence, hospitality, and respect for the importance of a once-in-a-lifetime event for many people.

While such thrills may come once in a lifetime, the desire to orchestrate them time and time again may be the very essence of a lifetime. It is often something that is bred in the bone— the outcome of local ties to family and to Notre Dame that span generations and take root in

Mike *(left)* and Elmer Danch

childhood. Mike's father, Elmer, a former local sportswriter, diligently followed the practice of the time by typing the play-by-play in the stadium press box for approximately thirty-five years worth of gamedays.

In addition to his work in the press box, Elmer Danch, as a Grand Knight of the South Bend Council of the Knights of Columbus, helped to start the tradition of hosting Friday night pregame Smokers that served to energize the city's male adults about each upcoming game. His journalistic work continued in the new millennium, with his articles appearing in the local diocesan newspaper, *Today's Catholic*.

Mike's mother, too, has connections to Notre Dame. One of her brothers played for Notre Dame as a Knute Rockne recruit. Another brother surpassed the fifty-year mark of serving as a stadium usher. Her three sisters became members of the Sisters of the Holy Cross.

Athletic Director: Kevin White

In September of 2006, the All-American Football Foundation honored several people from the University of Notre Dame at an event dedicated to President Emeritus Rev. Edward A. Malloy, CSC, and Director of Athletics Kevin White. Father Malloy received the Outstanding College President Award, and White was a corecipient of the General Robert R. Neyland Outstanding Athletics Director Award.

White has served as athletics director since 2000. He has held similar posts at other universities, and he has embraced the compatibility of sports with higher education, with the entirety of educational institutions, and with the whole person. He earned a PhD from Southern Illinois University specializing in higher education administration. He did postdoctoral work at Har-

Kevin White

vard University's Institute for Educational Management. He also has degrees in athletics administration and business administration. He has overseen a master plan that has rebuilt or is rebuilding facilities for many of Notre Dame's twenty-six sports teams, demonstrating stewardship over much more than football.

As director of athletics, White oversees not only Notre Dame's varsity sports program, but also the campus's extensive network of intramural sports, club sports, and recreation programs—a network in which most undergraduates participate. *Sports Illustrated On-Campus* ranked Notre Dame's intramurals program number one in the nation in 2004. In June 2007, White began a one-year term as president of the National Association of Collegiate Directors of Athletics.

Voices of Tradition: Mike Collins

Mike Collins, longtime co-anchor for the local news, loves television journalism, but he has a special place in his heart for his role as the public address announcer for Notre Dame football games. "I have the best seven-day-a-year job in America," he says. The games of 2006 marked his twenty-fifth season as announcer, and Notre Dame honored him by induction into the Monogram Club in a surprise private ceremony during halftime of one of the games.

Collins seems to have been destined for the position of public address announcer. He remembers when he was a young Pirates fan at his first baseball game in Forbes Field in Pittsburgh. "Suddenly, I heard this voice" echoing through the stadium, seemingly disembodied. "I was in total awe of that." From then on, whenever he would listen to a baseball game on radio, he

Mike Collins

would listen for the PA announcers, and he would mimic them. "I thought that was the coolest thing you could ever do, and I found out years later that it absolutely is."

Time passed, and Collins attended Notre Dame. He joined the student radio station WSND, where his duties included broadcasting pep rallies from the Field House. After graduation, he served as announcer for the hockey team. Then, in 1981, the former announcer for Notre Dame Stadium, Frank Crosiar, retired just before the start of the football season. Collins was asked to be the replacement.

"It was really nerve-wracking," Collins recalled. His first game was Notre Dame's first prime-time network night game. Since then, he has been the voice behind countless games and historic moments. He says he still approaches every game with excitement and passion, partly because he knows that some of the fans that day are in the stadium for their one and only Notre Dame football experience, and it has to be right.

He sees his principal duty as keeping the fans "informed and in the game"—without being a cheerleader, since the cheering happens naturally. "There's something so special about the Notre Dame football experience that being professional and enthusiastic is exactly what I should do."

One of his greatest memories—an "infamous moment," he says with a smile—is the end of the 2005 game against USC, the game that fans may remember as having two endings. It looked like Notre Dame had won. "I watch every game intensely with my binoculars, and I was certain the game had not ended," even though students had started rushing onto the field. He didn't have time to ask for permission. "I got on my microphone and, in the sternest father-like voice, I said, 'Get off the field *now* or your team will be penalized.'"

The students "turned as one," and regained a semblance of order. Collins says his wife later said it was like the parting of the Red Sea. "My mouth went agape. I never realized I had this much power." Of course, debates about the final outcome of the game (a 34-31 USC win) can and will go on, but Collins had done his job, and the Notre Dame students had listened. "I just wonder if they had that flashback"—to a prototypical experience from adolescence when they were scolded by their father—"and I hope they're not mad at me to this day."

From Collins's perspective as stadium announcer and Domer, he says the Notre Dame Stadium experience is different from that of many other places. For one thing, the tone in some other stadiums is disrespectful of the visiting team and its fans. "Notre Dame is big enough in so many ways, including its stature, that we should respect these teams and universities that come in to see us." At Notre Dame, when the visiting team makes a spectacular play, "I'm going to make sure people know." The overall hospitality shown toward visitors has them "leaving here with their eyes as big as silver dollars because of the way they've been treated for the weekend. . . . That's what the whole college football experience is about."

But Collins's particular loyalty and love for Notre Dame have only grown through the years, becoming "the fabric of my life." His younger son graduated from the university in 2006. His older son is the video coordinator for the football team. His wife's grandfather played for Knute Rockne.

"I represent Notre Dame on gameday, and I would never ever let them down," insists Collins. The professional way in which he has been treated by Notre Dame's administration "just means the world to me." When he reports to work on gameday, "I could be part of the team walking into that north tunnel. I'm going off to play *my* game today, too."

Voices of Tradition: Tim McCarthy

You've heard of the "long arm of the law," but fans in Notre Dame Stadium prefer to hear the funnybone of the law as delivered at every game, along with a serious message, by Tim McCarthy. It has been his job since 1960 to deliver a short message over the public address system reminding fans not to drive while intoxicated. He started doing this as a safety education officer of the Indiana State Police, but his quick caveats have remained popular beyond his retirement from the force and from a follow-on career in government. He's now in his 70s but still performing like a trooper.

The popularity (enhanced by NBC Sports in 2007) is due largely to the homegrown wit and the clever plays on words that he mixes with the warning against drunk driving. According to a *Notre Dame Magazine* article in 2000, some of McCarthy's personal favorites include these:

- "Anyone who tries to bolt through traffic . . . is a real nut."
- "No one relishes a pickled driver."
- "Keep your driving well polished to avoid having a bad finish."

More Voices of Tradition

NBC's many years of Notre Dame football coverage constitute a tradition in its own right, but there are other voices that have also come to represent the sport as practiced in South Bend. Fans listening on radio hear the familiar voices of Don Criqui '62 and Allen Pinkett '86 on the Westwood One radio network. Criqui succeeded

Allen Pinkett *(left)* and Don Criqui

Jon "JT" Thompson

Tony Roberts as play-by-play announcer in 2006, but he also broadcast Fighting Irish games for a period in the 1970s. Pinkett is a former All-American running back for the Irish.

The public address announcer for the Notre Dame Marching Band is long-time South Bend radio host Jon Thompson, known locally since 1975 as JT, as in his popular show, "JT in the Morning."

Stories that Stir the Heart: Jimmy Dunne

Notre Dame Stadium continues to be a magnet for all sorts of people with all sorts of stories. Often, they are stories that resonate with the metaphor of football—struggling through adversity with determination, as individuals and as a team.

Jimmy Dunne, a 1978 graduate and Notre Dame benefactor living in New York City, knew that the twin sons of his friend Chuck Witmer wanted to go to their first Notre Dame football game. During the 2006 season, he brought the boys, Andrew and Ian, to one of the games. Andrew had undergone surgery and radiation treatment for a malignant brain tumor the previous summer and had started chemotherapy that fall. But that was only part of the story of struggle and perseverance.

Chuck was one of the people who helped Jimmy put together the foundation that has been helping the families of employees lost from the investment banking firm Sandler O'Neill, where Jimmy is managing partner. Sandler O'Neill lost 66 of the 83 people working in its offices on the 104th floor of the south tower during the 9/11 terror attack on the World Trade Center. Jimmy and the foundation have helped to rebuild the firm while ensuring that the families of victims continued to receive compassion and financial support.

Jimmy and the boys met up with University President Rev. John I. Jenkins, CSC, on the fourth

Father John
Jenkins, CSC
(left),
university
president,
greets
(from right)
Andrew Witmer,
Ian Witmer,
and Jimmy
Dunne '78.

floor of the press box, the broadcast level. Father Jenkins blessed Andrew and said he would keep him in his prayers. That was one highlight the group mentioned later in a diary. Other reported highlights included the boys visiting Jimmy's old dorm, shaking hands with Brady Quinn and other players during the walk from the Basilica, and receiving a football signed by Coach Charlie Weis.

Stories that Stir the Heart: John Papaj

Usher captain John Papaj (pronounced pop-eye) loves to tell the story about the day he became a die-hard Notre Dame football fan. It was November 9, 1946, and he was a nine-year-old in Buffalo, NY, scanning the radio stations, when he picked up the Notre Dame-Army game from Yankee Stadium. He was just in time to hear Johnny

Lujack crossing the field to tackle Doc Blanchard, thereby holding the final score to 0-0 so that an undefeated Notre Dame team could go on to become national champions that season. "Once I heard that game, I was hooked," Papaj recalls. "From then on, whenever we played sandlot football, my team was Notre Dame, and I was Johnny Lujack."

Papaj stayed in Buffalo and retired from the General Motors plant there. In 1995, when he married his second wife, Sue, they honeymooned in South Bend. She knew of his love for Notre Dame and asked if he would like to move to South Bend. His affirmative answer prompted their move in 1996.

"When we first moved here, I used to walk the campus every day." He would touch the football and the championship ring on the statue of Frank Leahy outside the stadium. He would sit on the bench with the statue of Moose Krause.

John Papaj
at the
Leahy statue

He would touch the nose of Knute Rockne in the Rockne Memorial.

He started ushering for football in 1997 when the expansion of the stadium prompted a need for more than one hundred new ushers. Papaj has since become an usher captain and part of Cappy Gagnon's special-assignment usher squad. For the past several years, he has been posted on the University Level of the press box, seeing celebrities like Regis Philbin, Hank Aaron, Joe Montana, and many more.

He has gotten to meet Lujack and tell him his story. One of his favorite memories is escorting alumni of the 1988 championship Notre Dame football team from one of the corporate hospitality tailgates behind the Joyce Arena through the tunnel and onto the football field to be honored. "I had watched these guys win the national championship in 1988," he recalls. "Believe me, I had tears coming down my cheek. I could not believe it."

Papaj has ushered for every varsity sport except tennis and women's rowing. He has guarded the locker room for basketball teams and the Notre Dame dugout for baseball games. But, ever since hearing that game in 1946, he has a special place in his heart for football, and he has been able to express that through ushering. He expresses it by being one of the ushers willing to arrive at seven am to help guard the stadium. He was surprised the first time he received a paycheck for his efforts.

"We're like ambassadors for Notre Dame," he says. "We make everybody feel at home."

Symbol of Excellence: Chuck Lennon

"If you want to be good as a student or as an athlete, go someplace else. If you want to be great, come to Notre Dame." That's one of the memorable phrases—along with the ultra-memorable "Go Irish!"—identified with Chuck Lennon, executive director of the Notre Dame Alumni Association and associate vice president for University Relations.

He has been one of Notre Dame's strongest and most beloved bridges between all generations and segments of the university's alumni. His continually energetic performance leading cheers at pep rallies proves his ability as spokesman for—and symbol of—the spirit of the school to everyone in the extended Notre Dame family.

Lennon, a 1961 graduate, has also personified the school's connections of care and service to the surrounding community. Before returning to work at the university in 1981, Lennon was executive director of the Mental Health Association of St. Joseph County, the South Bend Model Cities Program, and the Community Development Agency.

Lennon and his wife, Joan, have five children: Sean, a double Domer (undergraduate and MBA degrees) who lives in Australia; Molly, a

Chuck Lennon leads a cheer at a pep rally.

1992 graduate working as the adidas representative at Notre Dame; Brian, a Harvard graduate, Marine Corps JAG officer, and 1992 Notre
Dame Law School alumnus; Colleen, a West
Point graduate; and Kevin, a Harvard graduate
and the vice president for membership services
for the National Collegiate Athletic Association.

In 2007, the Joyce Center Monogram Room
was filled for a tribute dinner celebrating Lennon's twenty-fifth anniversary as executive director of the Alumni Association. "There's no one
who better reflects what Notre Dame is about,"
said Frances Shavers, executive assistant to the
President. "He genuinely loves the students and
the University." Lou Nanni, vice president for
University Relations, declared Lennon to be "the
face of Notre Dame." He announced the establishment of the Charles and Joan Lennon Endowment for Excellence to benefit the Alumni
Association, the *Observer* reported.

Engaging the Culture with Excellence

Notre Dame's football players are learning, on the
way to leading. They're serving, on the way to
serving more effectively. They and their fans, in a
remarkable partnership that reflects Notre Dame's
ability to foster connections among people and
ideas, spanning time and space, project to the
world a sense of abundance and ambition, an ad-
herence to principles about the right way to excel.
The world responds to these attractive messages,
and it finds alternatives to the usual shortcuts
that only lead to cutthroat competitiveness, self-
absorption, and wandering in life's desert.

You might say Notre Dame's different road to
excellence and success is the scenic route, the
mindful journey. It's akin to the traditional trip

taken in the family car to visit friends and relatives. It entails many stories to be told, many games to be played, many thoughts and emotions to be relived, many purposes to be achieved, many talents to be celebrated, many virtues to be learned and lived.

This trip is taken every year (in football terms), actually every day (in personal terms). It doesn't stop with each intermittent victory or defeat. It keeps on going, in the context of something greater. One culture, comfortable and confident about its values and direction, intersects with a bigger, wilder culture, and the two become traveling companions, at least for a time, realizing they speak a common language. When the conversation goes deeper, the common language may occasionally fail, and words like "mystique" or "spirit" might have to suffice for explaining that more deeply rooted culture. Its participants—and all who can imagine new adventures and fulfillments worth experiencing and sharing—wind up wanting this family pilgrimage never to stop because it's a paradoxically joyful journey.

One example is seen in the little family trip that coach Charlie Weis took with his twelve-year-old son, Charlie Jr., immediately after the amazing 2005 game against USC, the heartbreaking Notre Dame loss marked by a disputed play as the clock ticked to zero. As reported by the Associated Press, "Weis tried to turn the disappointment into a teaching moment." The coach had his son accompany him in a walk to the USC locker room to congratulate them on their victory. "I just wanted to let them know that I had respect for their team and the way they played, and I thought that they showed a lot of character to go back and win that game," Weis was quoted as saying. "I thought it was a good lesson for my son."

Another example is seen in the life journey of Irish safety Tom Zbikowski, a skilled boxer who made his pro debut in Madison Square Garden in 2006. After a charity boxing event at South Bend's Century Center raised a large sum of money in March 2007, Zbikowski donated nearly $50,000 to a number of charities. According to the *South Bend Tribune,* his donations included $5,000 for the Make-A-Wish Foundation of Indiana, $2,000 for the Pediatric Brain Tumor Foundation, $1,000 for the South Bend Center for the Homeless, and $20,000 for Hannah & Friends.

"I was floored," Weis told the *South Bend Tribune* in April 2007 before his keynote speech to the South Bend Human Rights Awareness Day luncheon. This student had opted to give back as he prepared for another year of challenging football. "When we talk about college athletes off the field these days, a lot of times we're talking about kids doing bad things." Not so for Zbikowski, Weis was quoted as saying. "What he did, what this community did, is just unbelievable."

Excerpts from the letter, sent by Sorin to Moreau, are displayed on a sign located near the log chapel overlooking Saint Mary's Lake.

One cannot help but think of the Notre Dame football phenomenon as part of the providential, still-unfolding fulfillment of the hope—indeed, the conviction—of Rev. Edward Sorin, CSC, for the school he founded in 1842. That conviction was voiced in a famous letter that he wrote to Rev. Basil Moreau, CSC, founder of the Congregation of Holy Cross.

Sorin could not have foreseen the role of football in Notre Dame's relationship with millions

of Americans, nor could he have imagined the global growth of human and technological connections amplifying Notre Dame's exercise of good example. But he had the characteristic Holy Cross trust in divine providence and the spirit of perseverance that permeates Notre Dame athletics to this day. He knew that a powerful parable about God as a transcender of boundaries, the abundantly generous force forging and acting through relationships, was going to be preached for many decades to come as a result of the Holy Cross pilgrimage into the Indiana wilderness.

"As there is no other school within more than a hundred miles, this college cannot fail to succeed," Sorin wrote of Notre Dame in the Dec. 5, 1842, letter to Moreau. "Before long, it will develop on a large scale. . . . It will be one of the most powerful means for good in this country."

AFTERWORD

There is nothing like a football weekend when the Irish are fighting, and the gold helmets are hitting. Stepping on the field as a Notre Dame offensive lineman from 2002 to 2007 was every day a dream come true in my life. A lifelong Irish fan growing up, South Bend Saturdays held such a pedestal in my mind, and simply putting on that uniform brought forth several moments I will remember for the rest of my life. The feeling of a group of men coming together as one team with one goal is beyond my ability to describe, and that only begins the magic that seems to take place weekly.

I'll never forget the sound of the fight song as I marched up the tunnel after stretching, nor will I forget the sound of the crowd's cheers as our team sprinted out of the tunnel. That crowd became during my career more than a group of fans. In time, they became my extended family. Through the ups and downs of my life—on and off the field—they not only seemed to understand my trials, but also encouraged me to keep going, to keep pressing on towards the goal. My father passed prior to the 2006 football season, and I'll forever remember the outpouring of love, sympathy, and support that almost tangibly flowed from the stands. This family atmosphere

makes Notre Dame a place unlike any other around the country.

My experience at Notre Dame was laced with lengthy strains of individual growth and development, but none had more impact than the five-year process of commutative growth that I was blessed to be a part of. I was a naïve Southern Baptist boy from Texas, quite far out of my element on paper, but never more at home than I was on the third floor of O'Neill Hall or on the front line of Notre Dame's offensive team. Mr. Schmitt's discussion of our team's Fellowship of Christian Athletes huddle expresses my thoughts exactly as he describes the events with the statement "A Spirit that Transcends Religion." Though I've learned so much in my time growing up at the University of Notre Dame, seeing such a spirit in the midst of individuals and in the school as a whole was the most life-influencing development of my life.

I'm as proud as anyone to be a Notre Dame man. Not because of trophies, awards, or prestige that come along with wearing the gold helmets, but because that helmet represents every one of the behind-the-scenes intangibles that take place every weekend at the greatest place on earth. That title of "Notre Dame man" aided me in my pursuit of making a difference in the community of South Bend, our nation, and even the far reaches of our world. In the midst of my fifth year, I worked with Grace Church and have continued on staff there working with students in grades six through twelve. My time at Notre Dame played a large part in my choice to make a difference. Notre Dame did not open every door for me, nor did it force me to make any step I was unwilling to take. The impact of Notre Dame's influence in my life, however, is continually being felt, both by me and by those I encounter.

Bobby Morton

ACKNOWLEDGMENTS

So many people took time to talk with us about ways in which they knew of, and personally experienced, connections between Notre Dame football gameday weekends and beloved communities and traditions. In some cases, the assistance took the form of extensive interviews. In others, the help came in the form of reviewing texts for accuracy. In yet others, the help came in support and assistance for our photographic efforts and fact-finding endeavors of various kinds.

Special thanks to these employees of Notre Dame or its affiliates:

Dan Brazo

Dennis Brown

Drew Buscareno

Hilary Crnkovich

Michael Danch

Matt Dowd

Rev. Paul Doyle, CSC

Larry Dwyer

Steve Ellis

Ann Firth

Cappy Gagnon

Michael Garven

Amy Geist

Daniel Gezelter

John Heisler

Phillip Johnson

Mike Karwoski

William Kirk

Jennifer Laiber

Chuck Lennon

Michael Low

Patricia McAdams

Rev. James McDonald, CSC

Laurie McFadden

Kathleen McGowan

Jonette Minton

Jennifer Monahan

John Nagy

Clark Power	Kerry Temple
David Prentkowski	Chuck Van Hof
Rev. Kevin Russeau, CSC	Rev. Richard Warner, CSC
Kate and Steve Russell	Alan Wasielewski
Bill Scholl	Ryan Willerton
Henry Scroope	Todd Woodward
Gary Sieber	Jerry Wray
Matt Storin	Don Wycliff
Harold Swanagan	

Special thanks to these members of the surrounding community, or of communities geographically more distant, some of them having an affiliation with Notre Dame:

Dr. Stephen Anderson, MD	Kathleen McGowan
Greg Ayers	James O'Connor
Mike Collins	John Schalliol
Elmer Danch	Charles Sweeney
Jimmy Dunne	Dominic Vachon
Steve and Mary Filbert	Dr. Mark Walsh
Gene's Camera Store	Sally Wiatrowski
Gary Massapollo	

Special thanks to these Notre Dame students and alumni:

Sharon Bui	Brad Lenoir
Kevin Gleason	Nathan Menendez
Anna Jordan	Brooke Mohr
Mike Kelley	Chuck Vogelheim

Please forgive unintentional oversights where others generously provided valuable information and insights. Resources also included Notre Dame news releases and websites.

FROM THE AUTHORS

Lou Sabo

It was with great pleasure that I learned of and readily accepted the role of photographer for this book. The opportunity to explain and document the individuals and groups who are in various ways involved with game weekends has been rewarding—and a lot of fun.

While most are not on the field as members of the team, the individuals and groups in this book form a background of support, service, and enthusiasm that together benefits the community and gives everyone a chance to be a part of the excitement that is football at Notre Dame.

Growing up in South Bend, the son of a Notre Dame graduate who was on the freshman squad when Rockne was coach, I learned early the lore and legend of the game. I have also experienced first-hand the whirlwind of activities that takes place on game weekends in the city. I am always impressed by how many out-of-state visitors flood into South Bend for the games. This is a boon for the economy and an opportunity to showcase the city to the nation.

Photographing the activities and people in this book was an adventure, confronting extremes of location, lighting, and weather. I used film throughout because I believe in its superior image quality and capabilities. Traditional photographic processes also impart a certain "look" that gives a richness and depth well suited to documentary projects of this kind.

I would like to thank the University of Notre Dame Press for its help and cooperation on behalf of this effort. I appreciate the opportunity I have been given to photograph the many facets of involvement that Notre Dame football brings to individuals, the community, and the nation. I hope I have been successful in my work and you the reader enjoy this book, perhaps learn a few new things, and above all be entertained!

Bill Schmitt

I am a writer and editor in Notre Dame's Office of Public Affairs and Communication. My efforts to assist the University in describing its various programs and activities build upon more than two decades as a journalist, mostly covering subjects in business, science, technology, and government policy. I came to South Bend from the New York City area in 2003 to make a midlife career change with the very generous support of my wife, Eileen, who is my best editor in all areas of life. We shared a hope, since proven justified, that this move would be a good one not only for us but for our daughter, Mary.

As a Catholic who enjoys learning about the faith I practice and who strives with limited success to practice what I am learning, my enthusiasm about Notre Dame as a leading Catholic university was a major reason for making the move from New York. But the really distinctive and exciting character of Notre Dame came alive for me in a special way during the 2005 football season, when my duties included being down on the stadium field before kickoffs to assist with the tradition of flag presentations.

Stirred by the sights, sounds, and energy of the football games, I saw connections between the spirit of gameday weekends and the academic, religious, and social details of Notre Dame about which I enjoyed writing and in which I enjoyed being immersed. My background as a professed member in the Secular Franciscan Order helped me to appreciate the inspiring linkages that the Notre Dame football phenomenon makes between the secular and spiritual sides of human persons and communities.

Thus, the seeds of this book were planted, and I invited my photographer friend Lou Sabo to join me on a journey that would traverse virtually all the gameday weekends of 2005 and 2006, and some of the weekends of 2007. We sought to capture in pictures and stories many of the countless endeavors, traditions, community commitments, and individual passions that make these gamedays a unique contribution to people's lives and a joyful embodiment of the traditions and renewals of the amazing place called Notre Dame.